Treat Your
MARRIAGE
Like a
BUSINESS

Praise for *Treat Your Marriage Like a Business*

"Invest in this book! Mike distills his half century's worth of experience on how you can have a spectacular marriage. Mike has more years in the trenches of marriage counseling than I've been alive. No other person I know has more knowledge or expertise about the mysteries of marital success. Be prepared. Your marriage won't be the same."

– KOY ROBERTS, PH.D.
CHILD AND FAMILY PSYCHOLOGIST COPPELL, TEXAS

"In *Treat Your Marriage Like a Business* Mike has achieved what few others understand, much less can articulate. In a straightforward manner, Mike makes marriage improvement feasible for everyone. He uses proven coaching principles that enable spouses to enhance their marriages in a similar way to how great leaders enhance their business."

– MIKE HAWKINS
AUTHOR, *ACTIVATING YOUR AMBITION: A GUIDE TO COACHING THE BEST OUT OF YOURSELF AND OTHERS*

"Capitalizing on his 40+ years as a marriage coach, Mike Danchak brilliantly shines a light on the vital steps to success for couples experiencing a lack of intimacy and joy. Utilizing his extensive experience in the corporate world, Mike uses the concepts of success in business to reveal the path to success in marriage. His unique approach will appeal to men and women, which is rare in books on this subject. This manual challenges couples to get beyond the petty and discover the crucial elements that can derail marriages. Of the hundreds of marriage books out there it is the best that I have read. It should be in every married couples top ten books to read together, and is *must read* material for couples in crisis."

– JEFF NEIL
PRESIDENT, JN PRODUCTIONS

"Any on the go businessman or woman will find *Treat Your Marriage Like a Business* to be engagingly relevant. Using interactive coaching concepts Danchak brilliantly parallels business and marriage concepts. Mike's writing style will appeal to busy professionals who desire to improve their marriages."

– DES WOODRUFF
PRESIDENT/FOUNDER, GROK TRADE

"Mike Danchak is onto something! He has related healthy marriage practices to successful business habits. With twenty five years of experience helping management teams evaluate and improve their business relationships, I've concluded that there is little difference between success habits in the home or in the office. Mike goes where other authors have not by applying positive, measurable practices to improve marital health and encourage success. After the first chapter I was ready to take a fearless moral inventory of myself and my marriage. Applying Mike's insights had a positive impact on my personal and business relationships. Danchak's readable, relatable and doable information is for husbands and wives who desire to succeed at *Married Love*."

– LEROY HAMM
PRESIDENT, IHD CORPORATION

"We assumed that after six years of marriage and two children, we had a good relationship and didn't hesitate to partner with Mike Danchak to take an objective look at our marriage through the *Married Love Plan*. This thorough program revealed so much to us and ultimately allowed us to maintain focus on our marriage despite distractions and disruptions of life. For us maintaining focus includes scheduling quality 'couple' time and making candid open communication our priority. We continue to use the *Married Love Plan* to keep the emotional connection between us alive and growing and highly recommend the interactive coaching in *Treat Your Marriage Like a Business*."

– KYLE & LAUREN ETTER

"Mike used the *Married Love Plan* as the basis for our pre-marital counseling. What an amazing foundation to build our marriage on! We have consistently referred back to the truths and tools that we learned through the *Married Love Plan*. We enthusiastically recommend *Treat Your Marriage Like a Business* to other couples as a guide to prevent drifting apart as well as creating a lasting, enjoyable married life."

– Nick & Lindsay Zindel
Canopy Construction

"Mike Danchak has over 35 years of experience in family and marital counseling and coaching, much of this with corporate executives. Over that time, Mike has developed proven coaching methods that get results both in personal relationships as well as work place performance. His effort here is genius – getting people who are committed to growing their business to apply a similar strategy in their marriages. He has developed a unique coaching and counseling formatted approach that gives you intelligent direction and a plan to insure real change. Having benefited from Mike's work personally, this read is a must for those who want to get the most of their marriage. Get ready because he will make you work – work at something that is key to a happy, bountiful life!"

– Michael Fay
Vice President, Merritt Hawkins

Treat Your
MARRIAGE
Like a
BUSINESS

Coaching to Ignite Your Married Love Plan

Mike Danchak

**LEADERSHIP
PRESS**
LAKELAND
FLORIDA

To my wife Sharon,
my best friend, closest companion,
fun playmate
and the love of my life.

ISBN – 978-0-9828594-2-1
Library of Congress Control Number – 2010932145

Unless otherwise indicated, all Scripture references are from the
American Standard Version

Leadership Press
Lakeland, Florida

Book Design by: Daniel Crack, Kinetics Design, kdbooks.ca

**Attention Corporations, churches, universities, colleges and professional
organizations:** Quantity discounts are available on bulk purchases of Leadership
Press titles for religious, educational, business, fundraising or sales promotional
use. Special books, booklets or book excerpts can also be created to fit your specific
needs. For additional information, please contact Leadership Press, P.O. Box 7354,
Lakeland, FL 33807-7354 or mail@LeadershipPress.org

Printed in the United States of America

Contents

Acknowledgments

"No man is an island,
Entire of itself;
Each is a piece of the continent,
A part of the main."

These thoughts from John Donne's poem aptly express how this book came to be written.

Over the past years countless people have said, "Mike, you need to write a book." I want to acknowledge the effort and contributions of the following individuals who have been a source of motivation, encouragement, and prodding to get the job done.

Jeff Neil, in every step of the writing process has continually and consistently demonstrated in words and actions that he believes in me.

Scott Weinhold, for his probing inquires and honest feedback in the early stages of gathering information and writing the first drafts.

Joe Hawkins, for asking me to do on-site coaching and counseling with the MHA Group. This gave me the opportunity to understand the unique challenges of married corporate leaders by being a part of their day-to-day work life.

My editor, Greg Morris for support and patience in sharing his fresh insights, comments, and feedback that provided clarity, direction, and purpose.

To the married couples, past and present, who have provided insightful feedback and improved the quality of their relationships through *The Married Love Plan.*

I owe a debt of gratitude to a wide variety of psychologists, relationship experts and marriage counselors who have helped shaped my understanding, development, and practice of *The Married Love Plan.*

Preface

Treat Your Marriage Like a Business may sound cold and devoid of emotional connection, or is it?

Successful business is about working together to create trusting relationships in order to drive robust bottom lines. Building and maintaining a trusting relationship is also the keystone of a happy marriage. *Treat Your Marriage Like a Business* is a way of saying: "When couples work together to create an environment of trust, understanding, respect and mutual purpose in their marriage, they will experience a robust, intimate and emotionally connected friendship with one another that will last a lifetime."

Working as a professional development coach and counselor in the Dallas-Fort Worth metropolitan area has kept me in the trenches. I am regularly involved in the daily work and personal lives of countless couples from diverse cultural, socio-economic and professional backgrounds. These connections have afforded me the opportunity to appreciate the challenges and struggles of their frenetic lifestyles. These busy couples – the majority having children at home – struggle to keep their relationships out of the doldrums of marital drift, which if left unaddressed often ends in emotional emptiness, extramarital affairs or eventually, divorce.

I have discovered that a couple's need for relational improvement falls into three broad areas:

First, a commitment to the behaviors of love (i.e. understanding how to treat one another with respectful and need-meeting actions that create the feelings of being in love and being loved);

Second, to connect as friends (i.e. communicating in ways that strengthen the emotional connection of the relationship; conflict resolution that creates understanding and constructive behavior change, and casual conversation, laughing and having fun together); and

Third, sexual chemistry (i.e. candidly talking about unique sexual needs and desires, and regularly experiencing the excitement, variety and pleasures of the three kinds of marital sex).

Was it possible to combine my work experience as a corporate leadership development coach as well as a licensed marriage and family therapist into an effective plan to help couples improve their marriages? That was the challenge and so I developed a method to bridge the above two experiences into practical and doable self-directed coaching strategies: *The Married Love Plan: Commitment to the Behaviors of Love, Connected as Friends, and Sexual Chemistry.*

Treat Your Marriage like a Business: Coaching to Ignite Your Married Love Plan is not a scholarly book and therefore, I make very few bibliographic references. The relationship skills of the plan stand on the shoulders of the expert research and experience of countless behavioral specialists and psychologists. I have incorporated these skills into a couple's interactive coaching guide for *The Married Love Plan.* The book isn't long, but neither is it a quick read. *Treat Your Marriage Like a Business* is a toolbox of relationship information, personal assessments, checklists, questions, and Coachable Moments. These tools will assist you in spending the time needed in personal reflection in order to help you identify and then apply the coaching strategies to form specific behaviors; behaviors that need to stop, begin, or continue in order to make the necessary changes that will have a constructive impact on your spouse and your marriage.

With intentional and disciplined effort to drive the coaching strategies of *The Married Love Plan*, you and your spouse will develop actions that will express your understanding and appreciation of one another. These consistent and considerate expressions will ignite an emotional connection between the two of you that will keep the feelings of being loved and being in love alive and well in your marriage.

MIKE DANCHAK
LEWISVILLE, TEXAS
SEPTEMBER 2012

Introduction

*"Nobody can go back and start a new beginning,
but anyone can start today and make a new ending."*
– MARIA ROBINSON

If your marriage was a business, would you invest in it?

Would the forward earnings suggest sound management that could catch the attention of analysts and attract investors?

Would your business plan be based on proven principles that drive lasting results?

Would the organization's vision be flexible enough to adapt to the rapidly changing business environment in order to insure consist growth and a strong bottom line for years to come?

Would healthy benchmark relationship metrics indicate that your marriage would be a good investment?

According to current statistics on the state of marriages today, *40% or more couples' answers to those questions would be "no" — as their marriages end in divorce.*

A significant percentage of couples who stay together use the following phrases to describe their relationship:

Bland and dull
Dead and lifeless
Emotionally empty
Bumpy and rocky

Lack of intimacy
War zone
Failed communication
Destructive conflict
Headed toward divorce

Do any of the above phrases describe the current state of your marriage?

Treat Your Marriage Like A Business may sound cold and devoid of emotional connection, or is it?

Successful business is about establishing relationships in order to create a mutual purpose that promotes beneficial outcomes which drives a robust bottom line. In my coaching experience, business leaders frequently relate how multimillion dollar deals are often initiated and closed as a result of building trusting relationships on the golf course, the hunting or fishing lodge, the sail boat or over fine dining.

My wife and I recently dined at a restaurant at the Dallas/Fort Worth airport. The maître d' informed us that many high profile business leaders, actors, and athletes discuss and close major business deals while savoring a fine meal together. Developing relationships is critical in any business or industry. It fosters trust which forms the foundation for successful transactions. In fact, a large number of professionals leave organizations not because of a lack of business knowledge or performance but due to failed relationships with their peers, leaders or team members.

Building and maintaining a life-long trusting relationship is also the keystone to *married love*. Treat your marriage like a business and you can experience a robust, intimate, emotionally connected life-long relationship with your spouse.

Hollywood legend has it that Groucho Marx said the chief cause of divorce is marriage. That's like saying the chief cause of obesity is eating.

How is it that something so nourishing and enjoyable, so vital to our well-being can threaten our health?

How did the joy and wonder of that remarkable wedding day evolve into something we dread and regret?

What changed?

We live in a generation where men and women face unprecedented changes and lofty expectations for fulfillment in three major areas – family, work, and self. We are pushed and challenged to get it all: success, health, and happiness. I seldom meet a couple that reports a meaningful balance across their collective roles. Their laser-lane life styles create abnormal levels of stress, fatigue, and tension which lead to relationship burn out which all too often ends in divorce.

The Jared's careers had experienced a mercurial rise since their marriage eight years ago. Caleb was next in line to be CEO of the successful insurance company built by his grandfather. Lisa was an executive VP for the northeast division of a profitable and growing marketing firm. They had two children; one three, the other six, and all of the associated activities those age groups demand.

They were the American definition of success, with a collective annual income of $850,000. But as a result of the demands of their careers, combined with the challenge of being parents, something had to give. Their marriage did. Somewhere amid all these successful activities, they failed to notice the flames of their married love had been reduced to a few struggling, smoldering embers.

Caleb said, "We look good to everyone on the outside, but at home it's a different story ... constant sarcasm, criticism, and little, if any sex."

Lisa was more to the point, "We spend the best part of our energy and time 'out there' and have little to give to one another."

So if you were Caleb or Lisa, how would you fix this?

Caleb and Lisa's marriage was like many couples living in the fast lane of an upwardly mobile professional life. As a result of pursuing a successful career, giving their kids everything they thought they needed, and achieving their personal "goals," they neglected themselves as a married couple. It was the strangest type of self-sacrifice. They filled every part of their individual lives with whatever they wanted, except for treating one another with the essential behaviors that could keep the feelings of being loved and being in love alive in their marriage.

The joy and romance they remembered as newlyweds was now nothing more than a distant memory. Instead of being best friends and soul mates, they were isolated, lonely roommates living under the same roof as married singles. The tensions of life led to war words, insensitive actions, and the death of intimacy. They each built a wall around their emotional needs in order to avoid the pain of the feeling of being alone. The wall didn't remove the pain, it only served as a daily reminder of the emotional disconnect in their marriage.

Their marriage plan was a failure: failed management, failed growth and a failed bottom line.

For busy couples, the lack of intimacy often leads to an affair. The aftermath of the affair leaves the marriage shattered, filled with anger, bitterness, and guilt. The marriage suffers from a malignancy where trust, intimacy and communication are being eaten away. There is an emotionally empty or nonexistent sex life. They've already experienced an emotional divorce, and unless turned around, legal divorce is virtually inevitable.

So what about you?

Your marriage isn't that bad, is it?

Or have the passionate, emotional flames that once connected you and your spouse as one begun to die down?

Have things become a dull and boring routine?

Is sex a duty rather than a desire?

Maybe it's not even that bad.

Or maybe it's much, much worse … an affair.

If you viewed your marriage as a business, would it receive a "buy" or "sell" recommendation?

The good news is that if you want to change it for the better, you've come to the right place.

You absolutely can have the marriage of your dreams.

You can ignite your marriage and once again enjoy the warm and satisfying emotional connection of being best friends forever.

But is an exciting, upwardly mobile career and a "best friends forever" marriage possible?

You don't want to give up your career. You don't want to compromise on professional success. I get it.

But just as something changed with an obese person's eating habits to make them become unhealthy, something changed in your marriage to make it unhealthy.

So what do you need to change in order to turn your marriage around?

Whatever your business and regardless of your position in the organization, you know how critical it is to get correct information to implement sound management to position your career and company on the cutting edge in its industry sector. Companies with failed business models and dismal earnings, retain reorganizational specialists. The specialist's goal is to stop the downward drift and create a robust business plan that results in blow-out earnings. When making changes in your marriage, the same is true … you must have the correct relational information and guidance to drive the right behaviors that will turn the dying embers of a failed relationship into the passionate flames of *Married Love*.

Married Love Plan: Your Reorganizational Specialist

Most couples that end up in my office have successful careers and busy personal lives, yet their marriages are on the rocks. So I have developed a coaching approach tailored to meet the needs of their frenetic lifestyles. In the following chapters, I'll present relational principles and change strategies supported by current behavioral research as well as my forty-three years of successful experience in coaching busy couples turn their marriages around.

This is not a scholarly book and therefore, I make very few bibliographic references in the text. However, while this book is my synthesis of years of learning and experience, the ideas stand on the shoulders of many other counselors, coaches, psychologists, and researchers.

I've organized this wealth of relational information and my professional experience into a proven process, The *Married Love Plan*. Whatever state your marriage is in, *Married Love* can serve as the reorganizational specialist for your relationship. In the book, you'll be provided with a toolbox of knowledge and coaching strategies to help you better understand yourself and your spouse. These fresh insights will enable you to create an environment so you're both emotionally connected as friends and consistently demonstrating the caring deeds of *Married Love* that deliver outstanding relational results. As partners you will generate shared decisions and actions that will result in mutually experiencing intimacy, romance and the exciting pleasures of sexual chemistry. The struggling, smoldering embers can once again break into the flames of intimacy and passionate love.

The purpose of the first chapter is to provide you with an understanding of the *Married Love Plan*, the foundation on which the following chapters rest. I recommend you read chapter one at least twice before continuing with the remainder of the book.

Chapter two challenges you to take an honest look at the state of your marriage and how your own behaviors contribute to the current condition of your relationship. Plan to invest considerable time in reflection and introspection as you study chapter two. This can be a challenge since reflection, introspection, and meditation are nearly extinct in our frenetic lifestyle. The critical path to turning your marriage around begins with an honest self-assessment, which will lead to thinking about yourself and your marriage differently.

The assessments, questions, checklists, and coachable moments in chapters one and two, and throughout the book, are designed to help you identify problem areas and to drive the changes you need to make. They also serve as benchmark metrics to evaluate your progress.

For the sake of privacy, when taking stories from my practice, the names, places, and details are sufficiently masked to make them unidentifiable – except for one. The events of these marriages, however, are all true.

Through the following pages, I'll partner with you to ignite your marriage in order to create blow out bottom line relationship results. This approach works – but you will have to make the intentional decision to regularly execute on these behaviors in order to stoke dying embers into warm flames of married love.

"Americans believe in marriage and want to be married, but they haven't been educated about how to have a successful marriage," says CMFCE Director Diane Sollee (Coalition for Marriage, Family and Couples Education). "The good news," she adds, is that marriage "takes simple skills, not rocket science." *Treat Your Marriage Like A Business: Coaching to Ignite Your Married Love Plan*, provides those simple skills.

Put aside the romantic notion that love conquers all – and pull out your notebooks, planners and calculators. Successful partnerships require a plan, a CEO, COO, Senior VP of HR and regular progress reports.

To get you started on your *Married Love Plan*, here's your first coachable moment.

 *Coachable Moment*

1 Make reading and execution of *Married Love* your number one commitment during the next few months. Your commitment to make the intentional, disciplined effort to develop *Married Love* into a reality, is the first benchmark to measure the intensity of your desire to improve your relationship. Get a feel for the concepts in The *Married Love Plan* by skimming the pages of the book and having a quick look.

2 Give a second, slow and reflective read. This time through, complete the checklists, assessments, and Coachable Moments.

3 Carefully monitor your thoughts. There is a bias to rationalize thoughts that make us feel uncomfortable and challenge our current thinking and behavior. Be careful at this point. Rationalization enables you to discount information you need to hear and blame your spouse or someone else for the problems in your marriage.

"Coming together is a beginning,
staying together is progress,
and working together is success."
–Henry Ford

What Is Married Love?

"I used to believe that marriage could diminish me, reduce my options; that you had to be someone less to live with someone else when, of course, you have to be someone more."

– CANDICE BERGEN

*T*o those who have happy marriages, it may seem redundant. Being married just means being deeply in love. It's natural.

But to you, it sounds like an oxymoron. Being married means being in conflict. That's just the way it is.

The sad fact is that for many, being married does not mean being in love.

It's time to change that.

Married Love

As my dental hygienist was cleaning my teeth, she shared some of her marital challenges. I asked her, "How would you define *married love*?"

She paused and looked puzzled. "What do you mean by *married love*? I thought that love is just love?"

Like many couples, her understanding of what drives lasting love in marriage was fraught with distortions and a lack of correct information. So let's jump into the subject of *Married Love*.

Married Love is understanding your spouse in a way that enables you to do the very best for them. This is what married love *IS* (understanding) and what it *DOES* (actions). Love recognizes a unique value in the beloved and chooses to affirm that value with behaviors that sends the message:

I honor you as the most important person in my life

I respect you for the person you are

I want to understand you so that my behaviors meet your needs.

I want to be your best friend.

You make an intentional effort to know what your spouse thinks, feels and believes, and what causes him/her joy and heartache. Based on that understanding, you treat your spouse in ways that says, "*I value you above all else and only want the best for you.*"

Consistently treating your spouse in a way that conveys, "*I understand you; I know what you need to feel honored and respected. I value our relationship above all others,*" results in chemical responses in the brain that causes the feeling of being loved. These feelings drive the desire to be connected relationally (friends) and physically (sexual passion). As already mentioned, feelings and sex are a major part of love, but in marriage they are a *response to the way you're being treated by your spouse.*

Later, I'll give you detailed insights into how you can show honor and respect to your spouse and consistently trigger the "feelings" of romantic love and passionate sex.

*"One important aspect of a good love relationship
is what may be called need identification,
or the pooling of the hierarchies of basic needs in
two persons into a single hierarchy.
The effect of this is that one person feels another's
needs as if they were his own and for that matter
also feels his own needs to some extent as if
they belonged to the other."*

– Abraham Maslow

Married Love: A Diagram

Visually, *Married Love* can be communicated as in the following illustration. The three components are critical to your understanding of *Married Love*: Commitment, Connection and Chemistry.

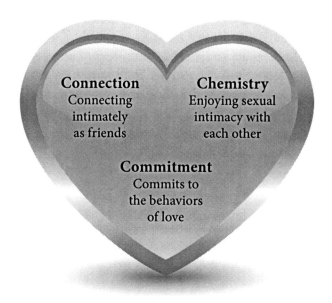

1. COMMITMENT:

being committed to the behaviors of love

This is the foundation of *married love*. Origins of unhappy marriages can be traced back to a failure to understand and consistently practice the behaviors that your spouse needs from you in order to have the feelings of being loved.

From birth, we've received different ideas and mixed messages about love from observing family, friends and our diverse culture. The messages are often confusing, distorted and flawed in some way. What we believe about love, true or distorted, impacts marriage in the following ways:

It colors our feelings towards our spouse
Influences how we treat our spouse
Affects our spouse's emotional state
Shapes the way our spouse treats us
Influences the way you feel

A major distortion is that love is just a feeling, or it's simply sex. If we don't have intense feelings or "red hot" sex all of the time, we think we are no longer in love. *Married love* does involve feeling and lots of sex. But neither feelings nor sex are foundational for *married love*; they're pleasurable by-products of how we consistently treat our spouse. In marriage, feelings aren't always as intense, and sex isn't always as passionate as we would like. *This doesn't mean our love is flawed!*

2. CONNECTION:

being connected intimately as friends

When couples consistently demonstrate the behaviors of love and doing the very best for the other, they become friends who make time to be together. When you treat your spouse in ways that makes them feel valued, affirmed, honored, and important, friendship is a natural result. When your spouse does something special for you, you think "*Wow, that was great.*" The *wow* thought results in a chemical response in your brain that creates feelings. These feelings or emotions cause you to want to spend time with your spouse. Doing things together, trips, walks, movies, transparent talks, sports, sharing, and talking together are a result of being committed to the behaviors that send your spouse the message, "*You're my queen, you're my king … I'm here to serve you!*"

Being intimately connected as friends is one of the things couples long for in their marriage, but often eludes them because they don't know how to make it happen. Friendship is the springboard to experiencing an intimate and romantic connection in your relationship.

The third aspect of *married love*, sexual chemistry, naturally flows out the emotional connection of friendship.

3. CHEMISTRY:
enjoying sexual intimacy with one another

Regular, exciting, passionate, and mutually satisfying sex in a marriage is built on the foundation of a commitment to the behaviors of *married love*. When couples are having sexual problems, I first rule out unresolved emotional problems from past sexual abuse and hormonal imbalances as the cause.

When neither of these are a factor, sex problems are a direct result of the lack of the daily demonstration of the caring deeds of *married love*. When you make an intentional effort to understand and consistently meet your spouse's needs, great sex is the natural result; it is the celebration of the health of the marriage.

Beware of this *Married Love* Killer

On a canoe trip down the Frio River in the Texas hill country, my wife and I came to calm waters and decided that this would be a nice place to take a break and have lunch. We stopped paddling, opened our picnic basket, and began to eat.

What we thought was a calm place in the river, was actually a tranquil pool that fed into swift, rocky rapids. As we enjoyed the beautiful bald cypress trees and riverbank ferns we focused on our meal but didn't notice the slow drift or the sound of the approaching rapids.

Then, what seemed like all of a sudden, the rapids were upon us! In panic mode, my wife screamed, "Mike, do something!" Instinctively, we both dropped our sandwiches and started furiously paddling to avoid the rocky rapids. Drifting disrupted our lunch and came close to turning over our canoe, dumping us into the cold, rocky rapids of the Frio.

Your career doesn't drift into success. You don't drift into a promotion. A successful project isn't driven by a drifting team, and you don't have consistent quarterly sales and earnings growth by a drifting sales force. It takes a savvy business plan driven by hard work.

The same is true for your marriage. A happy marriage isn't a drifting one; it doesn't "just happen." An emotionally connected marriage is built on sound relational information driven by intentional and disciplined hard work!

A drifting marriage will crash on the rocks of relational disaster. The question isn't, "*Will* it happen?" but, "*When* will it happen?" The danger of drifting begins the day you return from the honeymoon and you get into your daily routine. *Drifting is one of the most common and dangerous forms of marital failure.* It is subtle and quiet. It sounds no alarms. It just gradually creeps into your marriage. In time, the drift can destroy the emotional connection, and cause the marriage to end in divorce.

Many couples view marriage as a destination rather than a journey. You graduate; get a job; get married; have kids; build a career, a retirement account, and finally retire. At each of those stages, you apply your energies and accumulated knowledge to achieve the next goal. When the goal is simply marriage, you know enough to court your mate-to-be in a way that will create a strong attraction between the two of you. You win the heart of your beloved and get married. Then, with that win behind you, you move on to the next big goal: your career.

Your relationship takes a backseat and you begin to slowly drift away from each other.

The appearance of "all is well" is your placard. You fail to see the absence of real caring. Why should you see it? You have your preoccupations to keep you busy: career, hobbies, kids, recreation. The absence of emotional connection is accepted as normal. Due to this drift, communication slowly breaks down, you argue and fight over minor issues, blame is common, harsh words are frequent, you begin to look for ways to stay apart, intimacy is lost, and sex becomes infrequent, mechanical, or nonexistent. You act like casual or indifferent roommates, leading separate lives with little or no emotion. Your energies are focused on career-building and kid-raising.

Drifting is not an option for having an emotionally connected marriage! The only way you drift in a marriage is downhill into the disastrous effects of relational doldrums.

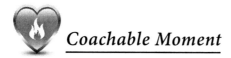 *Coachable Moment*

Let's have a drifting check up. How often do you and your spouse ...

1 Kiss goodbye when you part in the morning, and kiss hello when you come home in the evening?

____ Once a day ____ once a week ____ once a month ____ never

2 Talk about "us stuff" (your relationship) instead of family business (bills, kids, work)?

____ Once a day ____ once a week ____ once a month ____ never

3 Surprise each other with something special.

___ Once a day ___ once a week ___ once a month ___ never

4 Have a date night not involving other people or going to the movies?

___ Once a day ___ once a week ___ once a month ___ never

5 Make arrangements for a sleepover at a local hotel/motel?

___ Once a month ___ once every six months ___ once a year

___ never

6 Add variety to sex?

___ Regularly ___ seldom ___ never

7 Laugh together at something silly or foolish the other did or said?

___ Once a day ___ once a week ___ once a month ___ never

8 Rather than say a quick "Love you," you look in to each other's eyes, hold their hand and say with meaning, "I love you," as you give them a big hug and a tender kiss?

___ Once a day ___ once a week ___ once a month ___ never

9 Say "no" to a business associate's invitation to dinner, golf, etc., because you already have a commitment with your spouse and family?

___ Often ___ seldom ___ never

10 Tell each other your hopes and fears?

___ Often ___ seldom ___ never

The above are characteristic behaviors of *married love* and trigger the feelings of love. How often you express them is unique to each relationship. Give special attention to the *"never"* and *"seldom"* responses ... these are signs of a drifting marriage.

Is your marriage drifting?

Are you in the middle of treacherous relational rapids?

Has your marriage already crashed on boulders?

Are you willing to do the "hard work" it will take to turn your marriage around and keep it on course?

Married Love is a Team Effort

For our 25th wedding anniversary, my wife and I went to Costa Rica. The highlight of our trip was whitewater rafting down the Pacuare River, named one of the top ten river trips in the world by *National Geographic.*

As we drove up the mountain to our launch site, our guide provided instructions. He said, "Whitewater rafting is fun, exciting, and memorable. This is a trip you will never forget; however, the trip can also be dangerous and deadly. You will experience a couple of rapids rated four out of five, five being the most advanced and dangerous. People have been seriously injured, and even killed while whitewater rafting."

Well, that got my attention! He explained: "If the raft turns over, point your feet down the river with a slight bend in your legs to give you flexibility to push off the rocks. If your legs are stiff, the force of the current can break your legs as they hit the rocks. If you are caught underneath the raft, don't panic; point your feet down river to push off the rocks, feel your way to the edge of the raft, take a deep breath, and go under the water to get out of the capsized raft."

He continued: "When we are in the river, follow my instructions; do exactly what I tell you to do. When I say 'lean to the center,' immediately lean. When I say 'paddle once to the left,' I don't mean twice. I've been down this river hundreds of times.

I know every rock, boulder, current, and channel. I don't focus on the rocks, but on the currents and channels that carry us safely down the river. When you focus on the rocks instead of following the current, you end up crashing. I know how to navigate the river in order for you to have fun and enjoy the trip safely. Whitewater rafting is a team sport. If everyone follows my instructions, the current will carry you down the channels, we will avoid the boulders, and this will be one of the highlights of your life."

Well, there was rough water, boulders, and a couple of times we almost capsized, but everyone in the raft did exactly what the guide told us; we focused on going with the current and staying in the channel. The experience was everything the guide said it would be – an adventure of a lifetime! Eighteen years later, my wife and I still talk about our whitewater trip down the Pacuare.

Marriage and Whitewater

Like whitewater rafting, marriage is a team effort: husband and wife working together with a common vision. Similar to whitewater, there are dangerous behavioral rocks and boulders that can severely injure, and even destroy your marriage. But just like whitewater rafting, to experience the benefits of *married love*, you need a guide and must follow the guide's instructions. As you execute behavioral changes in order to drive the behaviors of *married love*, you will begin to slowly see a positive difference in the way you and your spouse respond to one another.

To put it another way, if you break both of your legs, you won't be able to run a marathon in three hours. All you will be able to do is hobble around on crutches with your legs in casts. As healing takes place and the casts removed, your walk is slow and uncertain. After the long, hard work of strengthening your leg muscles, you are finally able to run the marathon.

The same process holds true works in marriage. When you identify what's broken in your marriage, you'll be able to recognize what you need to stop doing, start doing, or continue to do in order to bring healing to your relationship. With patience and discipline, in time, you will be happily running the *married love* marathon.

How to Use this Resource

By reading and rereading this book, you will be guided through the steps of *married love*. When you answer the questions and consistently practice the *Coachable Moments*, you will begin to forgive yourself, forgive your spouse, and experience healing in your marriage. By regularly practicing these new behaviors, in time, you will experience the friendship and intimate emotional connection you both desire.

You will receive information based on sound relational research and my coaching experience with busy couples to help you understand and drive the behaviors of *married love*. The coaching and counsel in these chapters will guide you in multiple ways.

Thought Stimulator

To change direction in your relationship, you must first be willing to evaluate your current assumptions about self, marriage and career. Your thoughts drive your behaviors. Whether you agree or disagree with the ideas in the book, your responsibility is to implement strategic thinking skills to evaluate the coaching suggestions.

If you disagree, ask yourself, "*Why?*" Be specific with your response. "*I disagree with this because it will harm our marriage in the following way(s) ....*" Be careful that you don't rationalize. We consciously think, "*I don't understand why my spouse objects to my behavior.*" However, our unconscious brain thinks, "*I'm going to do what I want to do, regardless of my spouse's feelings and even if it hurts our marriage.*" Rationalization enables us to act on our self-serving/self-righteous/self-justifying thoughts without remorse.

Questions

Questions have the power to engage us and to shift our mindsets. They drive knowledge and growth, and fuel both creativity and critical thinking. One insightful question asked at precisely the correct time can alter the direction of your marriage. A Chinese proverb states, "He who asks is a fool for five minutes, but he who does not ask remains a fool forever."

As you've already noticed, there are questions laced throughout the text. Don't just read over the questions. Stop and reflect upon them. Verbalize your answers aloud. Listen to what you're saying. Sometimes just hearing what you're thinking makes you realize this isn't good for the marriage. As the wise sage observed, "Thoughts are clarified as they pass through the lips and finger tips."

Next, write your answer down. Read your responses a day later and give thought to what you've written. This oral and written process will help clarify your thinking and select specific behaviors you need to stop, start, or continue. This reflection is an essential step in developing self-awareness and helps you clarify and adjust your current thinking about how your actions are impacting your marriage. Once you have this clarity, you will be ready to initiate the behaviors of *married love*.

Accountability

Benchmarks along the way will help you assess how you're doing and what tweaks need to be made as you move toward your goal. Accountability is about asking the question, *"How am I doing?"* which helps you assess your progress in making needed and consistent behavioral changes.

When you determine what needs your attention, share it with your spouse.

"Honey, I know that my tone of voice has been sharp and often condescending when we've had different opinions. I apologize for

that and I'm committed to changing. This is what I'm going to do (describe what behaviors you are going to stop and start). Going forward, I'll ask for your feedback on how I'm doing. In fact, if we are in a conversation where my tone is inappropriate, just say 'time out.' That'll be a clue that I need to tone it down."

The questions, coachable moments, exercises, and the feedback from your spouse are the accountability components. The answer to the "how you're doing" question will be determined by your effort. It's easy to deceive yourself into thinking that simply because you're reading the book that you're working on your marriage.

Reading this book, attending seminars, or scheduling time with a coach or a counselor is meaningless unless you translate those experiences into a self-awareness that motivates you to drive the actionable behaviors in order to make needed changes.

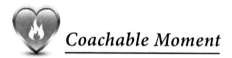 ### Coachable Moment

1   In your own words, give a definition of *married love*.

_____

_____

_____

_____

_____

_____

_____

2 Name four things you can do immediately in order to stop the drift in your marriage:

1 _____

_____

2 _____

_____

3 _____

_____

4 _____

_____

"Every day you spend drifting away from your goals is a waste not only of that day, but also of the additional day it takes to regain lost ground."

– Ralph Marston

Self-Awareness:
Married Love Begins Here

*"No stream or gas drives anything until it is confined.
No Niagara is ever turned into light and power until
it is tunneled. No life ever grows great until it is focused,
dedicated and disciplined."*
– HARRY E. FOSDICK

In my initial meeting with a couple, I begin:

*"You will make changes only if you believe they will be in the
best interest of your marriage based on your values. I will
be responsible for providing each of you tested relationship-
building concepts and skills to assist you in identifying changes
you need to make. I will coach and encourage you to make the
identified changes but I can't make you change … that's your
decision."*

At this point, they're both agreeable with what I've said so I
continue:

*"The first step in turning your marriage around is taking an
objective look at yourself and asking the question, 'What do
I need to stop doing or start doing to improve our marriage?'*

Coaching isn't about fixing your spouse; it's first of all about you making changes. When each of you commit to making needed changes, your marriage will improve."

It's at this moment I'll get resistance from husband, wife or both. In their minds, the majority of change in order to improve the relationship is the responsibility of the other. They think, *"My wife/husband needs fixing, not me!"*

For *married love* to turn your relationship around, you need to be self-aware of what changes need to be made in you, first.

Self-Awareness

Self-awareness is having a clear perception of your personality, including strengths, weaknesses, thoughts, beliefs, motivations, and emotions. Self-awareness allows you to understand how your behaviors either draw your spouse closer to you or drives them away.

Jerry's lack of self-awareness slowly destroyed his marriage.

Jerry: Leading sales rep for a major software company
Patty: Homemaker – married to Jerry for 14 years
Family: 2 sons, 1 daughter. Ages: 12, 8, and 4.
Marriage State: Lack of communication and intimacy, which creates tremendous emotional pain for Patty.

Main Points of Contention:

Jerry works all the time.
Patty feels emotionally abandoned by Jerry.
Jerry is overwhelmed by business responsibilities.
Patty is overwhelmed by the state of their marriage.

During my first meeting with Jerry, he explained that when he came home from a typical 12 hour workday, he noticed that the house was unusually quiet. When he went to get a beer, he found the answer for the quietness in a note on the fridge.

> *"Jerry, I'm done! I've begged you for the last time to make some changes in your work schedule. Your promises to make changes are empty. The only change you make is to placate me so I'll stop what you call 'griping about my job.' I'm tired of it! I don't know you anymore. I don't respect or trust you. You can take your money, house, and fancy car and go to hell with them!"*

There was a moment of silence. Finally Jerry said in a voice full of pain and confusion:

> *"Mike, what have I done? What am I going to do? I love Patty and the kids. I can't believe this is happening to me. I don't want to lose them! I didn't have a clue she felt so strongly about this!"*

Over the years, Jerry didn't hear Patty's pleas for change. Like many clueless husbands/wives, he lacked the self-awareness necessary to see how his behaviors had turned passionate flames into dying embers.

Developing a keen self-awareness is essential to understanding how your behaviors influence your spouse. You need to say to yourself:

> *"My spouse is giving me feedback on how my behaviors are negatively influencing him/her and our marriage. I need to listen to what he/she is saying and then give serious reflection on what I need to do differently. Once I have decided what needs to be done, I will make a commitment to change my behaviors."*

In his autobiography, *Be My Guest*, Conrad Hilton wrote that during his growing up years his mother repeatedly quoted two poets; Shakespeare and Sir Walter Scott. Hilton said that the ethical imperatives of these poetic lines formed his moral code during all the years that he built his hotel empire, sometimes to the consternation of his business associates. Not infrequently, when a business decision was on the table – "perfectly legal" but not necessarily ethical – Hilton would quote one, if not both, lines:

Shakespeare:
This above all: to thine own self be true,
And it must follow, as the night the day,
Thou canst not then be false to any man.

Scott:
Oh what a tangled web we weave,
When first we practice to deceive!

It's evident that these poets got it right. Whether in business dealings or in a marriage relationship — if we are first of all true to ourselves we will be true to others. Self-deceit is like a vicious dagger that cuts both ways: self-destructive, as well as destructive to our marriage.

The Joari Window and Personal Awareness

How do you get someone like Jerry to have an eye-opening moment to his marriage-derailing behaviors? What needs to happen to get Jerry to be true to himself? Patty has been telling him to change his work schedule in order to spend more time with her and the kids, but he hasn't heard. A tool I use that is helpful in developing self-awareness is Johari's Window.

Psychologists Joseph Luft and Harry Ingham (Johari) observed that there are aspects of our personality that we're open about and other elements that we keep to ourselves. At the same time, there are things that others see in us that we're not aware of, and a fourth window that neither others nor we know.

Public Knowledge Know to self Know to spouse	**Private Knowledge** Know to self Unknown to spouse
Unaware Self (Blind spots that eventually destroy the marraige) Know to spouse Unknown to self	**Unknown Self** Unknown to self Unknown to spouse

Problems in marriage come in the *Unaware Self* quadrant and are made up of consistent behaviors that damage the relationship. Spouses turn a deaf ear to feedback and as a result, are clueless to the negative impact their actions have on the marriage. The *Coachable Moments* and checklists in this book are designed to help you become aware of blind spots that eventually will destroy your marriage.

The goal in marriage is to have a growing amount of mutually held information in the public space. A healthy relationship is characterized by a public space that is free from deceit, misunderstanding, distractions, mistrust, confusion and unresolved conflict. The *Known to Self* and *Known to Spouse* space is grown through vigilant self-awareness, transparency, trust, safety, and good communication.

How do you get an unaware spouse like Jerry to stop long enough to think about the feedback they get from their spouse? What does it take to get a spouse to develop self-awareness? It's most often the pain of a traumatic experience, like coming home and finding your spouse and kids gone or discovering your spouse has had an affair.

The Jerry/Patty scenario is a frequent one in troubled marriages. The offending spouse gives a long list of things they've asked their husband or wife to change. When confronted with a crisis, the offender is often clueless and says, "I don't remember you asking me to make those changes." Or worse, the offender makes a short-lived effort at change, falls back into the same old patterns, and convinces themselves that they've made a lasting "change."

When failed attempts at change are consistently repeated, the spouse making the request gives up in disgust and distrust. The hollow promises and failures to follow through with change create skepticism towards any future pledges or attempts at change. The offended spouse thinks, *"Here we go again ... empty promises and lies ... this won't last!"*

Listen to what your spouse has been asking you to stop or start doing.

Careful here; selfishness can cause you to rationalize and allow self-justifying thoughts to deafen you to what you need to hear.

Learn to observe your own behaviors and notice how they influence your spouse's feelings and actions. What do your spouse's verbal and nonverbal responses tell you about how your behaviors impact him/her? If your spouse doesn't like what you're doing, step out of the experience and attempt to see it from their perspective. This isn't easy, but it will pay huge relational dividends.

 Coachable Moment

The following questions can start you on the path to becoming more self-aware, being true to yourself, and shedding light on your blind spots, the unaware self.

Take time to reflect on the following questions:

What are your thoughts about your spouse?

Self-observe how you talk and treat your spouse. Ask yourself, "What would I think and how would I feel if I were treated this way?"

Do I react to every little thing my spouse says and does?

Do I demonstrate self-control when my hot buttons are pushed?

What are my hot buttons? What do I need to learn in order to respond instead of react?

Am I impatient with my spouse?

Are my thoughts about my spouse critical and judgmental?

Am I selfish?

Do I keep my word?

Am I always truthful?

Do I listen to understand what my spouse is saying, or do I always butt in to express my thoughts and beliefs?

Do things have to be done my way or no way?

Do I complain about the way my spouse does things most of the time?

Do I assume I know what my spouse needs and what is best for him/her?

Do I have very high and unrealistic expectations of my spouse?

Am I a perfectionist?

Would my spouse say that I am kind, compassionate, and loving to him/her?

Do I look for the good in my spouse, or do I find faults and pick on them?

Do I appreciate my spouse for who he/she is, or do I try to change him/her into who I want them to be?

Do I live my life with integrity, honesty, high morals, values, and principles?

Do I honor the commitments and promises made in my marriage vows?

It's Not Fast Food

The Married Love Plan is not an "effortless, quick-fix, fast food" approach to building a lasting and intimate relationship. Your marriage didn't get into its present condition overnight and it's not going to change overnight. For some of you, it has taken years to develop the relational patterns that have slowly eaten away at the happiness of your marriage.

Married love is a process. It is a coaching approach that will help enable you to turn your new sense of self-awareness into relationship enhancing behaviors. *Married love* will help provide you with proven behaviors that will build a strong marriage relationship through developing a "how to" strategy/plan to implement these behaviors. The checklists and *Coachable Moments* provide benchmarks and metrics to evaluate your progress. Finally, guidelines for providing and receiving feedback with respect will continue to drive the needed personal changes to build a stronger marriage.

Now that you've begun to identify behaviors you want to change, you'll discover that you have a list of several things that need your attention. But how do you decide where to start? Couples often get frustrated with the challenging, and seemingly impossible task of making several changes at once. This frustration feeds a defeatist attitude and as a result, couples feel hopeless and often give up saying, "This is too hard and will take too long. I can't do it."

How do you deal with this dilemma? I coach couple's to use the term *cascading prioritization* to help them choose one high-impact behavior to initially change.

Here's how it works: a common stop/start behavioral request is listening. I hear Greg's words repeated many times in coaching: "Kara never listens to me. I need her to stop pushing her own agenda and for once, start listening to what I'm saying." By developing her listening skills, Kara's new behavior will have the following cascading impact on her and Greg's marriage:

Needed Behavioral Change	Listening Drives the Change
Greg needs to feel respected and understood.	When Kara listens, he feels respected and understood.
Greg feels like an isolated single in the marriage.	Kara's listening alleviates Greg's feelings of isolation and aloneness. He feels emotionally connected with Kara.
When Kara talks down to Greg, he feels stupid, lectured to and like a kid.	Listening creates a sense of equality with Kara. Greg feels that she respects him.
Kara always thinks she is right and Greg is wrong.	Kara's listening validates Greg's input and often causes both spouses to have a change of mind.

By working on one high impact behavior, couples notice not only the primary change, but also the cascading impact on other behaviors that need change. This cascading impact inspires a hope in couples that it won't take forever to turn their marriage around.

 Coachable Moment

With renewed self-awareness, you are now ready to take the *Married Love Check Up*. Check each one that applies to your situation and ask yourself, "What is going on (identify a specific behavior) in our marriage that caused me to make this selection?"

Pay special attention to number three under *Answer the Following Questions*. Remember what you've learned in this chapter regarding self-awareness.

Married Love Check Up

___ We have never been in love, not even when first married.

___ We have lost the love (emotional feelings) that we once felt for each other.

___ Frankly, I am no longer in love with my partner.

___ My partner is indifferent or seems to love someone else.

___ We do care about each other, but our marriage is dull.

___ I would like to know what I could do to improve our relationship.

___ I want to restore our love and save our marriage, but my partner is uncooperative.

___ My partner wants a divorce, but I don't.

___ We have serious problems but we agree on trying to save our marriage.

___ Due to my career, I don't spend enough time with my spouse.

___ Both of us want to learn how to keep the feelings of love and romance alive in our marriage.

___ Our marriage is good, but we want to keep it on course and growing.

Answer the following questions:

1 Name the four behaviors you most appreciate in your spouse. Statements must be positive and may include behaviors, attitudes, or personality traits.

1 _____

2 _____

3 _____

4 _____

2 From your point of view, the problem with your
   relationship is:

   _____

   _____

   _____

   _____

   _____

   _____

3 What is your contribution to creating the problem in
   your marriage?

   (*Hint*: The answer isn't, "None, it's all my spouse's fault.")

   _____

   _____

   _____

   _____

   _____

   _____

4 What is your spouse's contribution to creating problems
   in your marriage?

   _____

   _____

   _____

   _____

   _____

   _____

COMMITTING TO CHANGE

The *Married Love* coaching you receive will have a great impact on you and your marriage, if you will agree to the following commitment:

> "I commit to taking a serious look at myself and the way I treat my spouse. I want to become sensitive to how my behaviors impact his/her feelings. I will read the rest of the book looking for information I need in order to make necessary changes. I will call out my own selfish behaviors. Making changes won't be easy, it will be a challenge and it will take time and hard work. I'm committed to identifying and making the needed personal changes in order to be a catalyst in helping to turn our marriage around."

I will honor this commitment to change:

_____

Signature

_____

Date

"This above all: to thine own self be true,
And it must follow, as the night the day,
Thou canst not then be false to any man."
– HAMLET ACT 1, SCENE 3 WILLIAM SHAKESPEARE

My Most Important
Case Study

"When you are looking in the mirror,
you are looking at the problem.
But, remember, you are also looking at the solution."

– ANONYMOUS

*O*n occasion in this book, I will share case studies with you. All of these are actual people that I have coached. Of all of them, the following is the most important to me – because it is mine. I have never shared it until now.

CASE STUDY

> *Sharon*: Teacher, married to Mike for seven years
> *Mike*: Marriage Coach, Church Minister
> *Family*: One son, one daughter.
> *Marriage State*: Lack of communication, tremendous
>   frustration for the wife.
>
> *Main Points of Contention:*
> Mike is emotionally disconnected from Sharon.
> Sharon feels alone – like a "married single."
> Mike is busy with too many responsibilities.
> Sharon is busy with too many responsibilities.
> Their emotional connection has been put on hold, indefinitely

MY DRIFTING MARRIAGE

I've not shared this personal story until now. You see, many years ago, I almost lost my own marriage.

The summer I completed my graduate studies, my wife and I were married. We were so in love. We took long walks together. We looked forward to making love. We didn't want to leave the breakfast table.

Maybe you can remember those same feelings in your marriage.

But over the years, things changed. It wasn't dramatic. I became very busy with my marriage counseling practice and church ministry. My wife began work on her master's degree in counseling and guidance. Face-to-face time for us to grow in our relationship was slowly squeezed out by other priorities.

With the stress of schools, careers, and parenting, we slowly drifted apart emotionally. Our relationship began to suffer. We argued over the slightest thing, we could never agree on anything, and we looked for ways to be apart. The language of blame was common.

We were disconnected and living together as hostile roommates.

One day, my wife walked in the living room and said, "I've had enough." She told me she wouldn't leave me, but only because of her commitment. She wasn't in love with me. She said she felt like a "married single." She felt stuck in a "miserable marriage."

I was so involved with my own stuff, I didn't see this coming! At first, I was in shock and denial. Maybe I misunderstood. She couldn't feel "stuck in a miserable marriage." But she made it clear that she meant what she said! My shock and denial soon turned to anger. I said to myself, "I'm not that bad. If she wouldn't wear her feelings on her sleeve her emotions wouldn't be all over the place. I might need to make some changes, but so does she."

It took me a couple of days for my self-righteous indignation to calm down.

After two days of talking and crying together, we knew we didn't want a divorce and we wanted our marriage to last! We made a commitment to give our relationship top priority over the next twelve months. During those months we partnered with a marriage coach. The coach helped us spend time in serious self-reflection that allowed us to slowly learn and put into practice the three aspects of *Married Love*. At 43 years and counting, the intentional effort of *Married Love* is part of our daily routine that keeps us emotionally connected as best friends and lovers.

 *Coachable Moment*

Don't lose hope. Learn from us.

Whatever the state of your marriage, you can turn it around by making a commitment to do the hard work of learning and practicing the behaviors of *married love*.

> *"He that is good for making excuses
> is seldom good for anything else."*
> – BENJAMIN FRANKLIN

Forgiveness – Getting the Heart Ready for *Married Love*

"Love is an act of endless forgiveness,
a tender look which becomes a habit."
– PETER USTINOV

Stuff happens in every marriage ranging from forgetting to pick up the dry cleaning or failing to acknowledge your anniversary, to the intense emotional pain of having an affair. Some behaviors create miniscule discomfort, while others have a devastating tsunami effect. However, consistently repeated behaviors that overlook your spouse's needs, will eventually create hurt and pain.

When stuff happens, how do you keep the intense feelings of betrayal, anger, hurt or disillusionment from eventually destroying the marriage? How do you heal the hurt, stop the drift and ignite your marriage?

Seeking and asking for forgiveness is an essential part of the answer.

The first two chapters of this book encourage you to take an honest look at your role in the state of your marriage. The checklists, questions, and Johari's Window have provided you an assessment of how your behaviors influence your spouse's feelings and actions towards you. You should have a clear understanding of what you're doing that draws or repels your spouse.

Once you determine your role in the problems causing the drift in your marriage, you need to address the hurt and pain it has created in your spouse's heart. If you have been the offended spouse, you also need to address the pain in your heart caused by your husband or wife's actions. *Marriage is a duet, not a solo!*

Forgiveness becomes an issue in your marriage any time either spouse's actions (such as violence, physical/emotional abuse, a betrayal, a backhanded compliment, dishonest behavior, sexual infidelity) hurt, pains and dishonors the other. These actions cause you to experience hurt, anger, resentment, and bitterness. More often than not, the feelings drive a desire for revenge, getting even, and pay back. Unless these toxic feelings are managed, they slowly kill the love you have for your spouse.

Nursing the resentment and anger of an unforgiving spirit is a self-destructive act. Physician and author Dr. Gerald Jamplolsky has observed: "Hate, bitterness and vindictiveness are overpowering, self-defeating and intellectually as well as emotionally depleting." Or in other words, it would be similar to going to the store to purchase rat poison, ingesting it yourself and expecting it to kill the rats.

Forgiveness removes your desire to retaliate and frees you from the desire of revenge. With the poisonous and destructive emotions neutralized, you will be able to treat your spouse in a way that sets up an environment for the healing process to begin in your marriage.

Forgiveness Clears the Relational Track

Before a NASCAR race, there is a lot of activity on the track getting the cars ready. When it's time for the race to begin, the announcer roars, "Clear the track!" It's critical that nothing litters the track, as just a small washer could cause a car to spin out of control, wreck, and kill the driver. A clear and clean racetrack is a must to win the race.

In the same way, forgiveness clears the relational track in marriage. Forgiveness allows you to treat your spouse in a way that creates intimacy, romance, and friendship in your marriage. Learning and practicing forgiveness is not optional; it is necessary.

Forgiveness: the First Step to Reconnection

To begin the process of forgiveness is the initial step in repairing and restoring your marriage — it's the first move toward emotional reconnection. The bitterness of an unforgiving spirit keeps you focused on problems and continues to feed the sense of hopelessness. You say to yourself, *"I'm a victim, my spouse is the villain and I'm hopeless to do anything to make our marriage better."*

Before the seeds of emotional connection can take root, you must prepare the soil of your heart through forgiveness. Let me repeat that again – *Before the seeds of emotional connection can take root, you must prepare the soil of your heart through forgiveness.*

I've repeated this because some of you are thinking, *"I can't do this. How can I forgive? What my spouse did to me was unforgivable, he/she needs to pay for the pain and hurt they've caused."* Those thoughts are a natural response to the emotional pain you've experienced. However, if those thoughts are nurtured, the marriage is all but over.

Root Plowing

Root plowing is a process cattle ranchers use in South Texas to clear their pastures of unwanted brush. They do this so they can plant grass to feed their cattle. The process is simple. A bulldozer first uses a flat blade to knock down the brush. When that is complete, the dozer uses a claw-like blade that digs deep into the soil to plow up the roots. The roots and brush are then piled together and burned. The seed is planted in the fertile soil, the grass comes up, the cattle graze, and as a result, they are healthy and fat.

The same is true in a marriage: your heart must be ready to embrace the changes necessary to grow *married love*. Before that happens, emotional root plowing has to occur; the roots of bitterness must be removed. This isn't an easy process. Some of the roots are deep and take time to dig them out of the soil of your heart. Once your heart is cleared of an unforgiving spirit and the roots of bitterness are plowed and burned, you can begin to plant the seeds of *married love*.

FORGIVENESS IS A PROCESS

Forgiveness doesn't come naturally to anyone. You might be thinking, *"My spouse has hurt me and now you are asking me to forgive him/her? Instead of forgiveness, he/she needs to pay for what they've done to me!"* Forgiveness seems so unfair.

The natural desire for justice after our spouse has hurt us often leads to thoughts of revenge. Having vengeful thoughts is like playing an endless and painful video in our mind. It leads us to focus on the problem instead of forgiving and developing the relational habits of *married love*. An old Chinese proverb says, "He who seeks revenge should dig two graves." Not only does revenge harm the other person, it destroys the one seeking it as well. Revenge ends in the death of the actions that produce the feelings of love.

STEPS TO FORGIVENESS

Now, let's look at the steps you can take to forgive your spouse.

The first step in the process is to understand the meaning of forgiveness.
Forgiveness carries the ideas of "release," "sending away," or "letting go." The Greek word often translated *forgiveness* was used to indicate release from an office, obligation, debt or punishment.

Forgiveness is the mental and emotional process of releasing, sending away or letting go of the feelings of resentment or anger towards another. In your marriage, that means you give up the right to vengeance, perfection, retribution, and negative thoughts towards your spouse. Ultimately, forgiveness is a gift you give yourself, your spouse, and your marriage. It frees you from anger and resentment towards your spouse and empowers you to join hands in walking together.

The second step is to understand that forgiveness is not forgetting.
What you and your spouse have said and done to each other, both good and bad, will always be with you. However, forgiveness enables you to release the destructive emotions associated with the hurtful behavior.

An unforgiving spirit is like storing a barrel of toxic waste in your mind. The barrel is the hurtful behavior and it has a thousand tiny pinholes in it. The deadly waste is the painful emotions caused by the behavior. Slowly, the noxious pain seeps out of the pinholes and poisons your thinking, causing you to either strike out at your spouse or withdraw into resentful silence.

The emotionally healthy way to deal with hurtful events in your marriage is to get the feelings out in the open by talking about them. This initially may need to be with a skilled counselor or spiritual leader who helps you to get the process started. As long as your memory has an unresolved negative energy associated with it, it will eat at your spirit and slowly build a wall of resentment between you and your spouse.

As you talk, you will experience some intense emotions associated with the pain of the event. When you are hurt by angry words, physical and emotional abuse, lying, or an affair, you feel betrayed. Betrayal involves emotional loss and properly dealing with the loss involves grieving over it.

The third step of forgiveness is to allow yourself to experience emotions.
Part of the grieving process includes anger and sadness. Don't be surprised when you feel sad and angry as you work through the process of forgiveness. When you don't allow yourself to experience the feelings associated with the hurt and betrayal, you get stuck in the pain of the past and bitterness takes root!

The fourth step of forgiveness is making a decision to forgive.

When you have an understanding of the first three steps, you are ready to make the decision to forgive your spouse. Making the decision to forgive will allow you to begin releasing your anger and resentment toward your spouse. When you do this, you will slowly begin to experience the freedom of forgiveness and feelings of joy and peace will return as a result of the release of pent up hurts.

Once you've talked with your spouse, expressed the emotions, and have been understood with sensitivity and respect, you can then store the experience without the negative emotions. The barrel (remember the barrel is the experience itself and it is always a part of your subconscious memory) doesn't go away; but talking through the experience allows you to drain the hurt feelings (toxic waste) out of the barrel. When this happens, the event is no longer something you think about daily. When you see your spouse, the first thought is not the hurt, but the emotional connection you now enjoy.

Forgiveness is possible

Your emotional wounds may be so deep, that you might find it overly optimistic to think you can ever reach the point of being able to forgive your spouse. You understand what you've read, but you're just not sure you can do it. I understand … forgiveness isn't easy.

Sometimes it's helpful to hear about others who have been able to forgive after suffering seismic emotional wounds. Like the Minneapolis mother whose only child was shot dead. She showed the ultimate forgiveness by inviting her son's killer to live next door.

Or consider the Burundi national who forgave the criminal who burned her three aunts. She went as far as to visit him in prison. She declared: "Hate kills, but forgiveness frees the soul."

These people did not come to the decision to forgive immediately; but they did reach it, and so can you. Forgiveness is a change in the thoughts, emotions and behavior of the offended spouse. It is letting go of the anger and bitterness towards your spouse. It liberates you from desiring revenge and clears the way for you to develop the habits of *married love*. When you forgive your spouse, it also creates an environment for him or her to acknowledge their wrongs and begin to change the way they treat you. Forgiveness creates a relational environment where you can develop the emotional connection of *married love*.

The Responsibility of the Offender: Acknowledgement, Apology and Change

Forgiveness addresses the responsibility of the offended spouse. But what about the responsibility of the offending spouse? For a broken relationship to be restored, it takes not only forgiveness on the part of the offended spouse, but the offending spouse must acknowledge their hurtful actions, sincerely apologize for the behavior, and change the behavior going forward.

Forgiveness frees the offended spouse from bitter feelings. However, for the relational playing field to be cleared of all the debris and reconciliation to occur, the offending spouse has the responsibility of acknowledgement, apology, and repentance. Until this happens the offended spouse will find it difficult, if not impossible, to trust. Without trust on the part of the offended spouse, there is little hope for an intimate relationship.

Acknowledgment
When the time is right, say to your spouse, "When you have a moment, I would like to share some things with you."

Find a time when you can be alone, not interrupted by kids or the cell phone. Spend time in reflection before you have this conversation. Don't have the talk if you are not emotionally ready. The delivery of what you want to say will hold more weight than the specific words you use. If this comes across as manipulation or self-justification, you're dead in the water! Your spouse will sense your sincerity, or your lack of it.

When you acknowledge your hurtful behavior, say something like, "There are things I have done that have hurt you." Specifically list behaviors your spouse has repeatedly told you that are offensive. This transparency helps your spouse see that you are self-aware and that you accept responsibility for your hurtful actions.

Apology

Immediately follow the confession with a sincere apology. The dictionary defines an apology as: a written or spoken expression of one's regret, remorse, or sorrow for having insulted, failed, injured, or wronged another. Apologizing serves to initiate in the heart of the offended spouse the process of dealing with the intense negative emotional baggage caused by the hurtful action. Apologizing is the restorative centerpiece that sends the message to the offended spouse that mistakes have been made and there is an *intention to change!*

And then you say nothing. Don't explain or qualify your comments. To do so only risks saying something that will dilute your response or cause your spouse to question your intent.

A change in behavior

After an acknowledgement and apology, the next step is a consistent and lasting change. The word *repentance* captures the essential meaning of change: "to undergo a change in frame of mind or heart, which results in a turning around, a consistent change in behavior." The spouse who repents has a change of heart that translates into a change in behavior. The offending spouse talks with the offended spouse and discusses and agrees on behaviors the offending spouse needs to stop or begin. When you repent, your changed behavior demonstrates the sincerity of your apology to your spouse.

The process of acknowledgment and repentance is at the heart of rebuilding trust in your marriage. Infidelity and deception create uncertainty in the relationship. To rebuild trust, you must accept responsibility for what you have done, ask for forgiveness, change your behavior, and here is the kicker ... be consistent in the new behavior.

Acknowledgment, apologizing, and consistent change are relational healers that drive reconciliation.

Brad, married for 35 years observes: "Forgiveness has kept Beth and me together. There have been times over the past 35 years that we both have said and done things that have hurt the other. It took us a while to learn the necessity of acknowledging our misdeeds to one another and changing our behavior, but forgiveness and owning our own stuff has kept the feelings of being loved in our marriage and have kept us out of divorce court!"

 *Coachable Moment*

Forgiving

1 Read this chapter at least three times to clarify the meaning and process of forgiveness.

2 Identify what your spouse has said or done that has hurt you. Ask yourself, "What has been keeping me from forgiving my spouse?" The answer to this question is found in a thorough understanding and application of the steps of forgiveness.

3 Begin the process of letting go and healing by applying the steps of forgiveness.

Acknowledgement/Apology/Consistent Change

1 Carefully follow the guidelines for acknowledgment, apology and change. Failure here derails the entire forgiveness process and speeds up the destructive drift in your marriage.

2 Schedule times to talk with your spouse to make sure your behavior is aligned with the "change discussions" you've had.

> *"Forgiveness doesn't make the other person right,*
> *it makes you free."*
> – Stormie Omartian

Suggested Reading:

Forgiving the Unforgivable, David Stoop Ph.D. Ventura, CA: Regal Books, 2005.

To Forgive Is Human: How to Put Your Past in the Past, Michael E. McCullough, Ph.D., Steven J. Sandage, M.S. and Everett L. Worthington Jr., Ph.D. Downers Grove, IL: InterVarsity Press, 1997.

What's Love Got To Do With It?

Love is a look, a smile, brief as an instant,
long as eternity, a spark engendered by a
reaching out, a touch of hands, an intuition
that knows how to heal a hurt, and how to build a world.
For love's sake only, cherishing each other,
lovers move freely within a circle, that
defines their being, shapes what they become,
and thus they are fulfilled each in the other.

– AUTHOR UNKNOWN

*T*here is a lot of confusion as to what love means.

I love football.
I love cheesecake.
I love my kids.
I love … you.

I often ask the following question in seminars: "How would you define love?" I then have participants complete this sentence:

Love is _____
_____ .

Now you complete the sentence: Love is _____
_____ .

I get all kinds of different answers. Love is:

Sex
Friendship
Compassion
Sympathy
Romance
A sensitive attitude
Family
Having kids

So, what do you think?

It is no wonder people are generally confused about the meaning of love. It is one of the most overused, under-defined words in the English language. And popular culture gives us so many mixed messages — in movies, TV shows, romance novels or advertising. Love can be defined as just about anything.

Defining love in this culture is like trying to see air or hear thoughts.

A DEFINITION OF LOVE

Love is most often thought of as an emotional experience or intense feelings we simply fall into when the time is right.

It's something we have little or no conscious power over — it just happens. We dream of falling in love; it requires no effort on our part.

The truth is, "falling in love" is primarily a combination of physical appearance and body chemistry.

When I've asked couples, "What initially attracted you to your spouse?" I've received all kinds of answers.

"He/she was cute."
"He had a silly looking car."
"I liked the way she smiled."
"He looked cute in his bellman's uniform."
"He was funny ... handsome."

"I liked her hair."

"He had great muscles and a cute face."

Now, I don't want to downplay physical attraction. It is important.

Here's how physical attraction, body chemistry, and "falling in love" work:

Someone catches your attention. Your thoughts trigger a chemical response in your brain, resulting in feelings. This feels good, so you do you what you can to repeat the process that makes you feel good.

Do you remember first falling for your spouse? Those late nights talking on the phone? The infatuation? How every thought was dominated by the possibilities of this new relationship? Skipping sleep just to be together, thinking about each other, doing things for each other? Your heart felt like it was going to explode as you went for the goodnight kiss.

You even looked for creative ways to express your love. You gave each other gifts. The gift said, "I know what you like, I know what you need and I'm going to do all that I can to give that to you."

When you were first dating, what did your spouse do that caused you to have the feelings of love? It feels good to remember those times, doesn't it?

This first look, the physical attraction that triggers the feelings of "falling in love," is captured in the lyrics of *Some Enchanted Evening* from the classic musical, South Pacific.

Some enchanted evening
You may see a stranger,
you may see a stranger
Across a crowded room
And somehow you know,
You know even then
That somewhere you'll see her

Again and again.

Who can explain it?
Who can tell you why?
Fools give you reasons,
Wise men never try.

INFATUATIONAL LOVE

During the infatuation phase of new love, the experiences and feelings of love motivates you to give to the person you love. Your giving to each other creates a strong emotional bond and connection. You finish each other's sentences, you understand each other's likes in a way no one else ever has, and you both know that you have met "the one."

Who can explain it? Who can tell you why? Fools give you reasons, Wise men never try.

An enchanted meeting ...
Dating ...
Engagement ...
Marriage ...
Honeymoon ...
Happily ever after ...
And then ... real life.

Uh-oh.

After you return from your honeymoon, it's back to a life of work, maintaining a household, and paying the bills. Reality.

Behaviors and personality traits not revealed during the dating or through the honeymoon period begin to reveal themselves now. The self-deception created by the intense emotional fog of that enchanted evening has lifted. This new person you have just noticed, the one you have been blessed with, is also the one you promised to live with "until death do us part!"

You feel trapped.

Your future is dominated by responsibilities, the needs of your kids, and the demands of your role in your family.

And somewhere along the way, you realize that those intense feelings of infatuation love are a distant memory. Now, not only do you not feel them, you don't think you're even capable of feeling them ever again!

The Chemistry of Infatuation Love

Physiologists believe that somewhere after one and a half to two years (or less), the natural stimulants that bombard our systems during new love lessen. The intense emotions are no longer felt. As a result of not understanding the natural changes in body chemistry, you think you are no longer "in love."

When this happens, couples often come to me for coaching, saying, "*We don't feel the way we once did.*"

They're right.

The change in the intensity of feelings causes panic to set in.

"We love each other, but we're not IN love. Is our marriage over?"

"When we were dating he would buy me flowers at least once a week, but he doesn't anymore."

"When we first met, she told me how strong and handsome I was. Now she complains that I'm developing a pot belly."

When this is talked out in a coaching session, they realize they still like being around each other even though they have their ups and downs, but the feelings of "new love" or infatuation or no longer there. Since the intense feelings and the behaviors driven by those feelings are no longer present, they wonder if they've married the wrong person or if the marriage is over.

Remember, during the infatuation phase of new love, the experiences and feelings of love motivates you to give to the person you love, to understand and meet their needs. Your need-meeting behavior of giving to each other creates an emotional connection: the feeling of being *in* love.

The lyrics of *On the Street Where You Live* from the classic musical, *My Fair Lady* capture the intensity of emotions in infatuational love. Note the highlighted words.

> I have often walked down this street before;
> But the *pavement always stayed beneath my feet before.*
> All at once am I *several stories high.*
> Knowing I'm on the street where you live.
> Does *enchantment pour out of ev'ry door?*
> *No, it's just on the street where you live!*
> And oh! *The towering feeling*
> Just to know somehow you are near.
> The *overpowering feeling*
> That any second you may suddenly appear!
> For there's *no where else on earth that I would rather be.*

Married Love

So how do you define your love now?

How do you keep the feelings alive after years of marriage?

This is where an understanding of *agape* (the Greek word for love) love helps us move from infatuation love to committed *married love.*

Infatuation happens only once. It's like that ride at Disney World that seemed so magical when you were seven.

But don't get discouraged. The good times are not over.

You can have frequent, intense, exciting, intimate and romantic feelings in your marriage — even after the fourth year.

In fact, you can have them all the way till death severs your relationship.

You just need to understand and practice *Agape Love* or what I call *married love.*

Agape Love is

A willful decision
A deliberate conquest
An unconditional commitment to meet the needs of
Giving honor and value
Acting in the other's best interest in spite of their behavior

It is how Jesus knew you could "love your enemies."

Agape love is doing what's right because it is the right thing to do, not because you feel like doing it. If feelings of being hurt and taken advantage of form the basis for your actions, you would strike out at the person who treated you that way. However, because they are a human being, you treat them civilly, even though you don't like (have positive feelings towards) them and they have done you wrong.

Agape is love defined and driven by conscious choice. It is not driven by feelings, thus you're able to demonstrate need-meeting behaviors to someone whose behaviors make them seem unlovable.

In marriage, it is a deliberate choice to meet your spouse's needs even when their behaviors cause you to want to lash out at them with hurtful words and actions. You make a willful choice to override your emotions by doing the right thing, even though you don't feel like it. (Review the *Married Love* Diagram in Chapter One).

Is Married Love Impossible?

If you have children, you know how to love someone who does not show love back to you. When the newborn arrives, its name is *"I don't care what you are doing … what time of the night or day it is … I want, I need, give it to me right now!"* So you patiently feed this new arrival every two to three hours, you change it, you wash it, you cuddle it, you comfort it, and you burp it so it won't have a tummy ache.

After doing all of this, the newborn says, "Thanks mom and dad for being so considerate," and gives you a big smile.

Yeah, right!

Our feelings for our kids will never be about what they give and do for us. We love our kids because we value them. We protect and nurture them. As parents we give to them for 5, 10, 15, 30 years. Unconditionally.

If you've got kids, you know.

If you don't, you will when you have them.

You use *Agape Love* to love your kids.

Assessing and Appreciating Value

Your kids come into this world with important needs, needs that are your responsibility to fulfill. If you don't fulfill those needs, you could lose that child. So you work hard. You lose sleep. You sacrifice so that your child will have a life better than the one you experienced as a child. It all seems so natural, but in reality you have trained yourself to do this because it is the right thing to do.

When you sacrifice for something, work so hard for something, when you make your main focus the nurturing and protection of whatever that something is, you come to value it.

Jesus observed, "Your heart will be where your treasure is" (Matthew 6.21, *God's Word Translation*). *Agape Love* is the ability to value your spouse in that same way. Your spouse is your treasure and as a result, you treat him or her with honor.

Married Love is about making a willful choice, a willful decision to treat your spouse right, even when you feel like treating them wrong – even when they've done something that hurts us.

It's time to make a choice about your spouse.

You have to make the choice of whether your primary focus is getting your own needs met, or giving to your spouse so their needs are met.

Each of us has a "getter" and a "giver" part of our personality. When your needs go unmet, the "getter" causes you to do whatever you find necessary in order to get your needs met and to feel happy or fulfilled. You demand, manipulate, cry, scream, beg, lie, or cheat in order to get some of those needs fulfilled. Whenever getting your needs fulfilled comes at the expense of dishonoring your spouse, you may experience temporary satisfaction, but your relational needs – the need to feel loved and valued by your spouse – will be left unfulfilled.

Maybe your "getter" behaviors are causing the current dissatisfaction you're experiencing in your marriage.

Feeling loved by your husband or wife transforms influence on your relationship. But how does this happen?

It begins by placing value on someone beyond you. It is through fulfilling your spouse's needs that you create the loving experience in your heart. When you have that experience in your heart, you feel ultimately fulfilled. Not only do you feel fulfilled, but you are no longer needy. Giving to your spouse will also inspire your spouse to see value in you and to willingly fulfill your needs. As soon as you bring your "getter" under control and begin to focus on your spouse's needs, you get everything! You get the experience of feeling loved that comes only through giving. Now, because you are focused on fulfilling your spouse's needs, your spouse ends up being concerned about fulfilling your needs.

This is why the Scriptures say, "When you give, you will receive."

IT'S TIME TO GET YOUR M.B.A.

Dave Thomas, the founder of Wendy's, once appeared on the cover of their annual report dressed in a work apron with a mop and a plastic bucket in hand. Here's how he described that picture: "I got my M.B.A. long before my G.E.D. At Wendy's, M.B.A. does not mean Master of Business Administration. It means Mop Bucket Attitude."

Dave Thomas' *servant attitude* will give you tremendous power to change the course of your marriage. Here's how:

Understand serving creates value.

You value what you nurture and care for. The power to change the course of a relationship begins with serving and that ultimately creates value. You create value in your marriage by serving your spouse.

Look for ways to serve your spouse without being asked.

To do this, you must understand your spouse, what your spouse needs and what your spouse would appreciate. My wife often prepares food late at night for our meals the next day. When she finishes, it is late and she is tired, so she goes to bed without cleaning up the kitchen. I know she likes a clean kitchen in the morning, so I will get up early and clean up the mess she made the night before. I don't like doing it, but I like her. Take some time every day to look for little ways to serve your spouse that sends the message, "I value you, I know what you need, I want to serve you, I love you."

Don't expect your spouse to say, "thank you"
or do something for you in return.

When I clean up the kitchen often times my wife says, "Thank you." But other times, she doesn't say anything. I do it anyway because I know that's what meets her needs. It is my way of saying, "I love you." The servant spirit acts in the best interest of the other person with no expectation of reward.

In a difficult marriage, don't expect your spouse to immediately give to you because of your servant spirit. Be patient, behavior change takes time. You need to be careful here, because at this point you may be tempted to become resentful and harbor bitterness. Avoid thinking that your service is never noticed. And don't serve with the intent to manipulate your spouse to get what you want. Give because it is the RIGHT thing to do, regardless of your spouse's behavior. Remember that selfless giving – in time – can soften your spouse's heart.

So exactly what is agape love?

What does it look like in real life?

Agape Love is:

- Purposeful action taken to discover and create value.

- Unconditionally loving your spouse when their behaviors are unlovable, undeserving, and unresponsive. You treat them with honor and respect, even though their behaviors may cause you pain.

- A permanent commitment to your spouse. Commitment in adverse relational circumstances reflects your understanding of agape love, that you will love your spouse for better or worse.

- Constructive, purposeful giving – not based on sentimentality or manipulation, but on knowledge and a willful decision; the knowledge of what is right and what is in the best interest for your spouse.

- Consistent need-meeting behavior. When your spouse does not reciprocate, it would be easy to grow weary and give up trying. Agape love is patient and kind in the midst of the most difficult circumstance. This caring love shows an ever-present concern by serving the other.

 *Coachable Moment*

At the beginning of the chapter, you were asked to complete the sentence, "Love is _____." Now that you have read this chapter, complete the sentence again and compare the two. What is different about your first sentence and the last? Now, write a brief paragraph on how this chapter has impacted your understanding of love.

Based on agape love (*married love*),

1 Identify three behaviors that are currently doing harm to your marriage. Commit to stopping these behaviors.

1 _____

2 _____

3 _____

2 Identify and initiate three need-meeting behaviors that will demonstrate that you understand and love your spouse.

1 _____

_____

2 _____

_____

3 _____

_____

Love never gives up.

Love cares more for others than for self.

Love doesn't want what it doesn't have.

Love doesn't strut,

Doesn't have a swelled head,

Doesn't force itself on others,

Isn't always "me first,"

Doesn't fly off the handle,

Doesn't keep score of the sins of others,

Doesn't revel when others grovel,

Takes pleasure in the flowering of truth,

Puts up with anything,

Trusts God always,

Always looks for the best,

Never looks back,

But keeps going to the end.

– 1 Corinthians 13, *The Message*

Suggested Reading:

Love is a Decision: Thirteen Proven Principles to Energize your Marriage and Family. Gary Smalley and John Trent, Ph.D. New York: Pocket Books, 1993.

Keeping The *Feelings*
Of Love Alive

I climbed up the door and opened the stairs,
Said my pajamas and put on my prayers,
Then I turned off the bed and crawled into the light,
All because you kissed me goodnight!

– Sandy Rolstan (*attributed*)

*B*rian and Sammy were scared and broken hearted. They expected that their marriage that began with "enchanted evening feelings" would continue as a "until death do us part" relationship. Yet after just fourteen months, all that had changed. Brian put it bluntly, "Mike, we like one another but we no longer love one another. We think we've married the wrong person."

I responded, "You like but no longer love one another? What does that mean to you?"

Sammy quickly jumped in: "Brian is a super guy. He is honest and works hard, but I no longer have the feelings I once had for him. I hate to say it Mike, but I no longer love Brian."

Brian responded, "As much as I hate to say it, I agree with what Sammy said. I like Sammy, but I'm no longer in love with her! We've been married less than two years. We both hate to throw in the towel, but neither of us can stay in a loveless marriage. The feelings we had at the beginning are no longer there. Is there any hope?"

Sammy and Brian were in the transition from chemical infatuation (refer back to the discussion in chapter five) that drives behaviors that create the feelings of love, to *married love* where consistent caring behaviors create the feelings of being in love and being loved.

Like many couples they didn't know the difference between infatuation love and *married love*. The driving force between the two is 180 degrees. As a result of Sammy and Brian's lack of knowing, they were unable to make the transition from one to the other. This left them panicked, thinking there was no hope for their marriage.

The key to keeping the feelings of being loved and being in love in a marriage – even when you are on a demanding career path – is practicing *married love*.

Love begins in the mind. It is not simply an emotion that rises spontaneously in our hearts; it has to do with the will. It is a decision, a conquest, a victory, an achievement. Finding a perfect, flawless person does not create *married love*.

Married love is created by one imperfect person (you) meeting the needs of another imperfect person (your mate). By getting to know your spouse, you are able to give to them in a way that touches their core being. It creates the connection and feelings of love between you.

The foundation of *married love* is to give to your spouse in a way that meets his/her needs. When his/her needs are met, your spouse will have the feelings of being loved and honored and will respond by meeting your needs in return.

Sounds simple, doesn't it? Contrary to what some would have you believe, you don't have to be a genius, a rocket scientist, or a psychologist, to understand how *married love* works.

It does require a committed discipline to consistently demonstrate behaviors to your spouse that make them feel valued.

That may cause you to think, "If my marriage takes that much work, maybe I made the wrong choice."

You didn't think that when you repeated your vows. At that moment, you most probably valued your new mate more than virtually anything, maybe even your own life.

In our discussion on the definition of love, we established that in order to put love for your spouse first, you need to develop a servant spirit.

A servant honors and serves one of greater value. A servant doesn't ask, "What's in it for me?" but, "What can I do for you?"

So, in order to have a servant's spirit, you must confront your own selfishness. A materialistic, entitled mind-set makes it very difficult to develop a selfless, servant spirit.

This reminds me of a little sign a couple gave me after completion of their coaching sessions that read, *"The most difficult years of marriage are those following the wedding."*

We spin our selfish nature to ourselves in a way that convinces us that everything is okay. Because our eyes are focused on "my way," the marriage begins to slowly drift away from a focus on the relationship. Drifting is not an option if you desire to have an emotionally connected marriage. The only direction you drift in a marriage is away from one another.

Couples often explain this drift or lack of feelings in their marriage with, "We have problems in our marriage because we are not compatible."

THERE ARE NO COMPATIBLE COUPLES

Why do I say that? As I just mentioned, each of you has a nature that is "my way" centered. Frank Sinatra wasn't the only one who did it *My Way*. Most divorced people did, too.

A "my way" attitude is a major enemy of *married love*. It clouds your judgment, it causes you to filter your marriage vision for your own interest, to rearrange your priorities to suit your own needs, to blame your spouse for your marital problems and if not brought under control, will erode the foundation of your marriage. Instead of considering how your decision impacts your marriage; you spin your choices to make it sound like it's in the best interest of your relationship.

Compatibility is created through:

Grace. This means you give your spouse what you don't think he or she deserves. Perhaps it's forgiveness, understanding, a second chance, or a listening ear.

Mercy. This means not giving him or her you think they do deserve. Perhaps this includes criticism, punishment, harsh words, or retaliation.

Disciplined effort to demonstrate the graceful and merciful actions of *married love.*

You and your spouse *can* be compatible

You must make the decision that your spouse is Number One and everything else will revolve around your marriage.

Here are some essential behaviors that drive the thoughts and chemistry that keep the "feeling of being in love and loved" alive in your marriage.

Patience

Patience is the ability to endure waiting, delay, or provocation without becoming annoyed or upset. It is the ability to persevere calmly when your spouse does or says something that irritates you.

The husband of one of my coaching clients was always on time and his wife frequently ran late. He would tap his fingers loudly, grow angry, and pace anxiously while spewing stinging barbs at his wife.

He had learned to wait. That's something. Now he had to learn to wait patiently.

Forced waiting and fuming silently feeds anger. Through coaching, he learned that patience and a good attitude go hand in hand. He began to demonstrate patience by realizing the *value* of his wife ... by deciding that his wife was worth the wait. After he could do that, he began waiting calmly. Meanwhile, his wife, who ran perpetually late, learned to make an effort to be on time. When she wasn't, she learned to show patience with her husband's various expressions of impatience.

In my marriage, I've discovered that patience means biting my tongue when I feel like wagging it. For many years, I thought that telling my wife my every thought – as I was thinking it – was constructive communication.

Turns out, it was destructive because my wife wasn't ready to hear all of that. It actually pushed us further apart. When I learned to calm down, to listen more than I talked, and exercised patience, things began to improve.

Patience sends the message, *"Yes, your behavior has frustrated me, but I love you anyway. I'm going to show you that I love you by controlling my tongue and temper."*

 *Coachable Moment*

1. Pinpoint the triggers that often influence you to lose your patience.

Impatience creeps in insidiously, and if you feel anxious, worried, or unhappy, you may not even realize that the underlying cause of these feelings is impatience. To reduce the frequency of impatience, it helps to be aware of it. What actions or words used by your spouse always seem to influence you to lose your cool? Sit down and make a list of all the things that your spouse does that cause anxiety, tension, or frustration. At the core of most triggers is a reality that we have a hard time accepting our spouse. Remember, *married love* emphasizes accepting and serving your spouse, not changing your spouse.

2. Overcome bouts of impatience.

In the long run, developing patience requires a change in your attitude about life. But you can immediately begin to make progress by learning to relax whenever you feel impatient. Take a few deep breaths and just try to clear your mind. Concentrate on breathing and you'll be able to get your bearings.

3. Look for patterns.

Being aware of your impatience also gives you the opportunity to learn from it. Perhaps you can uncover thoughts about your spouse that simply are not healthy or constructive, thoughts that you may have the power to change. Figure that out, and you can then think logically about the problem issue and decide whether or not your impatience is warranted or helpful. It usually isn't, but when it is, you can figure out ways to fix the root problem rather than simply feeling stressed about it.

4. Let go if you can't do anything about the impatience trigger.

If there isn't anything that you can do to resolve whatever has triggered your impatience, just let it go. Easier said than done, yes, but it is possible, and it's the only healthy thing to do. Some things about your spouse may never change. Remember: it is not your responsibility to change your spouse; it is theirs. You can respectfully share your thoughts and that's it. If you make a concerted effort to be more patient in relatively inconsequential, short-term situations, you'll gradually develop the strength to remain patient in even the most trying and enduring situations.

5. Remind yourself that change takes time.

People who are impatient insist on getting things done *now* and do not like to waste time. However, some things just can't be rushed. Think about the happiest memories in your marriage. Chances are, there were instances when your patience paid off, like when you took a little extra time to spend together.

6. Remember what matters.

Not focusing on what matters most in your marriage fuels impatience. Move your marriage toward the goals of *married love* by honoring your spouse, being kind, acting generous in forgiving your spouse, being grateful for what you have, and taking full advantage of what matters most. When other less important things fuel our impatience, taking time to remember any one of these items reduces our tendency to want something different at that very moment.

Kindness

Kindness is giving your spouse attention and encouragement that result in a feeling of being special and valued. It is treating your spouse in a way that nourishes their esteem, builds them up, and motivates them to be their best.

Bryan comes home after a rough workday. The project he's been working on around the clock for weeks hasn't come together. After a tense meeting with his concerned boss, Bryan heads home fatigued.

When he opens the door to greet his exhausted, six months pregnant wife, he is confronted with, "I sure hope you won't work all hours of the day like this when the baby is born!"

Without saying a word, Bryan watches his wife take the meal out of the oven that she had been laboring over for the last few hours. He knew he was desperately in need of something, but couldn't put his finger on it.

Then there is Amy, a mother of three, who has also had a rough day. Shortly after her husband, Travis, left for work, one child developed a fever. After a stressful day of serving as both doctor and mom, Amy is preparing dinner when her husband enters and says with a smile, "The house looks like a disaster area. What in the world did you do all day?"

Not returning the smile, Amy becomes defensive as she sets out his dinner. She also needs something, but feels too overwhelmed to express it.

What Bryan and Amy both needed was kindness. Bryan needed a hug and a, "I'm so glad to see you, I know how tired you must be after all that!" Amy needed her husband to notice her overwhelmed state and come to her aid.

Every spouse needs kindness daily. Many of us feel that life is like an overworked, fast-moving engine. In mechanical terms, an engine receives a constant supply of motor oil to prevent friction and overheating. Likewise, random and intentional acts of kindness lubricate marriage relationships, easing life's friction.

An offer to help, a smile and a kind word will reduce the heat of everyday responsibilities. Knowing that your spouse cares enough to notice and say "thank you" makes the day-to-day routine a little easier to handle.

In essence, kindness is shown in your marriage when one spouse *chooses* to use his or her strength in a gentle manner to meet the needs of their spouse. It genuinely causes their mate to feel loved, valued, and honored.

Did you ever have a doctor who was quite knowledgeable about medicine but had a poor, impersonal bedside manner? The doctor may have been quite insensitive to your world and experiences. In fact, his behavior may have even created anxiety and tension on your part.

In the same manner, all the knowledge that you have that your spouse might need to hear is ineffective if you deliver it in an insensitive way. You show kindness to your spouse through the words you speak and how they are spoken.

Mark Twain declared, "I can live for two months on a good compliment."

The writer of the Proverbs in the Bible remind us that "the tongue has the power of life and death ... an anxious heart weighs a man down, but a kind word cheers him up."

Out of insensitivity, we begin to be gruff, sarcastic, or demeaning in response to our spouses' normal questions. Our answers appear sharp instead of seasoned with sensitive understanding. Learn to respond to every question your spouse asks with respect, and demonstrate that respect by taking time to give a sincere and sensitive answer.

Spoken kindness is also expressed in the selection of words, pitch, rate of speech, and our body language. All of these create the tone of our delivery. It is possible to never say a wrong word, yet communicate an unkind attitude when we speak. You are the loudest and most consistent voice your spouse hears. It's your choice to use a kind voice that supports and encourages your spouse, or a gruff voice that discourages, degrades, and minimizes.

The words you speak and the way in which they are spoken will soon become the heart of your everyday lifestyle. Be intentional about talking with your spouse several times a day. The purpose of "kind talk" is not simply to speak words, but provides another tangible way to connect with your spouse and express your love.

 ## *Coachable Moment*

1 Mother Teresa, the Roman Catholic nun and Nobel Peace Prize winner asserted: "Kind words can be short and easy to speak, but their echoes are truly endless." Here are some *kind word* primers you need to use on a daily basis:

Thanks for doing _____ .
I like the way you did that.
I appreciate your help with _____ .
Please.
Is there anything I can help you with today?
Thank you.
Let me get that for you.
I like it when you _____ .
Thank you for showing me another perspective.
That (mention a specific) was neat. It made me feel very special.
I really appreciate your thoughtfulness with/ when you _____
_____ .

Wow, you look beautiful/handsome (When you complement your spouse, avoid generic generals. Be very specific: "You look handsome in your shirt, pants, suit ...," Your blouse brings out the beauty in your eyes," "I love your new hair-do, it makes you look sexy, exciting ....")

2 The following "blame talk" phrases don't express kindness and need to be avoided at all cost:

You need to stop!
Why don't you?
If only you would ...
You don't care!
You are selfish, controlling, hateful, inconsiderate ...
You should ...
You ought to ...
When you start ...
You never listen to me.
Don't you know?

Kind Touch

One excellent way to keep the feelings of love alive is through touch. In her book *Anatomy of Love*, anthropologist Helen Fisher describes the importance of touching in general: "Human skin is like a field of grass, each blade a nerve ending so sensitive that the slightest graze can etch into the human brain a memory of the moment."

Numerous studies show that the emotional health of a baby is greatly affected by how much positive, physical touching they receive early in life.

In the same way kind touch is critical to building romance and intimacy in your marriage. And husbands, I don't just mean touch as it relates to sexual play.

I'm talking about a tender touch while your partner is doing almost any ordinary task. A gentle squeeze on your wife's shoulder as she is preparing a meal or a soft rub on your husband's back as he is reading a book can communicate loving messages in ways our words never could. There is simply no more eloquent way to say ...

"You are not alone,"
"I appreciate you,"
"I'm sorry,"
"I love you"
than through touch.

Because physical touch is so important to *married love*, you need to talk about it. You may have come from a touchy/feely family and perhaps your spouse didn't. You have the right – and the responsibility – to determine what's normal and comfortable for you.

Take time to explore with one another how touch was used in the home you grew up in. This simple conversation can provide a much better understanding of how and why the two of you may have different touch quotients. It can also show you how you both can better understand the use of kind touch in your relationship.

It's the small everyday gestures of kindness and love that will fortify your relationship. If you don't do the little things, then the big things are just so much fluff. That grand gesture will seem very hollow if the kind talk and kind touch aren't part of your everyday behaviors that sincerely say ...

"I care about you ... "
"I honor you ... "
"I'm so thankful that I married you."

In a one-on-one conversation, Andy shared, "My wife loves having her scalp massaged. Many nights she falls asleep with me reading, holding my book with one hand and massaging her head with the other. She knows I'm not trying to manipulate her into something more, and I know it's something she truly loves and feels served by—in spite of the shoulder pain or my arm falling asleep!"

The following random acts of kindness capture the spirit of kind words and kind touch:

Say "Good morning!"
Ask how he or she slept.
Make something for him or her to eat.
Help find something your spouse misplaced.
Check with your spouse to make sure they have everything
*   they need for the day (money, food, information, etc.).*
Call during the day just to say hello.
Run an errand at the store.
Listen and comfort your spouse if he or she is upset.
Help your spouse with his or her tasks at home.
Speak gently and respectfully.
Do favors.
Spend time together before going to sleep.

Showing kindness to your spouse is fundamental to marriage. Kindness is contagious. Being kind to your spouse creates goodwill and cooperation. When you are kind, your partner is far more likely to be kind to you. Emotional closeness, appreciation, and love will grow stronger and stronger with each act of kindness you and your partner show each other.

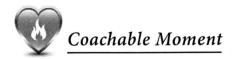 *Coachable Moment*

Three simple things you can do to drive "non-sexual touch" in your marriage are:

1 Hold hands when you go places together; in the movies or when walking in the mall. Hold hands.

2 Hug each other in the morning as you begin the day and in the evening as you end the day. A big bear hug!

3 Give each other a kiss in the morning and at the end of the day and say to each other, *"I love you."* Make this more than just a peck on the cheek!

I can hear the moans, "I can't do that, I just don't feel like it!" Would you possibly do something (hug, hold hand, a kiss in the morning) that initially feels uncomfortable for the sake of achieving something far more valuable in your marriage?

If you've been working on yourself beginning with the first chapter, by now you should begin to experience some small changes in the way you behave – and *feel*. I know that the above behaviors are difficult if you are not used to doing them. They are especially difficult after years of emotional separation. However, countless couples, even though their feelings were not initially aligned with their behaviors, have consistently practiced these behaviors and their emotions changed from indifferent and angry to the feelings of loving and being loved.

Humility

Feeling loved needs a spirit of humility to stay alive in your marriage. In *Married Love*, humility is being authentic, being real with your spouse, and discarding the false masks of "I know it all." Humility has to do with submitted willingness. It involves a healthy self-forgetfulness. Self-forgetfulness is a foundational concept that drives the servant spirit of *married love*. Humble spouses don't think less of themselves, but think more about their mate. An arrogant spouse is puffed-up, self-absorbed, and focused on their own needs instead of the marriage.

There are numerous benefits to practicing humility:

It nurtures and grows the behaviors that drive the feelings of loving another and being loved.

It reduces anxiety. You don't worry if your spouse is going to cut you down because he or she doesn't agree with you.

It encourages more openness and paradoxically, it enhances self-confidence.

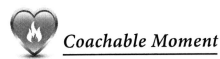 *Coachable Moment*

1 Here are several ways to demonstrate humility to your spouse:

Be selfless, putting your spouse first
Be consistent with small acts of service
Welcome advice from your spouse on many topics and problems
Be quick to admit when you are wrong
Accept apologies and offer forgiveness quickly and freely
Respond graciously when you are really right and your spouse is wrong

2 Keep in mind the twelve humble words to remember in any heated discussion:

"You are right."
"I was wrong."
"Please forgive me."
"I love you."

Now, when you say these words, don't harbor resentful feelings. You have to really mean it, and in moving forward, back them up with the way you treat your spouse.

3 Avoid lecturing, preaching or giving unsolicited advice to your spouse. Stop and listen to your spouse. Remember,

you don't have to always add your unrequested or uninvited thoughts. When in doubt, ask questions.

Respect

Respect or honor is treating your spouse as the most important person in the world. The original definition of honor literally meant something that was heavy or weighty. When we honor someone, we are saying that they carry weight with us and they are extremely important to us. Honor is a decision we make that declares our spouse has great value.

"But what if my spouse doesn't deserve honor or respect?"

To this point, our emphasis has been that behavior change is a two-fold process: first in the mind and then in the actions. Your response to your spouse can change dramatically once you've made the decision in your mind that he or she is truly valuable, in spite of their behaviors. There will be times in your marriage when you are motivated to honor your spouse, not out of their behavior or the way you feel, but as an act of your will; to treat them civilly and with respect because they are a human being.

Keep in mind, honor does not dissolve healthy boundaries by allowing your spouse to hurt or harm you in any way. Honor is not an absolution of all your spouse's faults, nor is it a promise to be less than honest about their destructive behaviors. It is a behavior. This is not an easy process, and may be a topic you should discuss with a professional marriage coach.

 *Coachable Moment*

Try these ways to demonstrate honor:

1 Respectfully listen to your spouse's opinion, advice, and beliefs without making critical remarks.

2 Give your spouse your full attention when they communicate with you. Put down the newspaper or turn off the television while they are talking with you.

3 Curb the practice of any distasteful habits in front of your family.

4 Avoid over-committing to other projects or people that take you away from your family on a consistent basis.

5 Allow your spouse the freedom to think for him or herself without any attempt from you to dominate or curb their free expression of thought.

6 Know your spouse. In what additional ways can you demonstrate honor to them?

Honesty

Honesty is being free from deception and is the bedrock of your marriage. It is essential for trust, for building compatibility, for creating a way of life that you both enjoy, and for maintaining the feelings of love in marriage.

"But we are honest!"

How honest are you? Is there a line you can draw which marks where a little bit of secrecy turns into dishonesty? Is there such a thing as "mostly honest?"

Being honest is like being pregnant. You either are or you're not.

There is no halfway. In marriage, partners must learn to become completely honest with each other if they are to achieve true intimacy.

"You lazy thing, all you ever do is sit around and look at trash on television, you never do anything to help keep the house picked up!"

That's not being honest. It's being rude and disrespectful.

"I'm overwhelmed with things I need to get done, and I'm wondering if there is a way you would be willing to help me out?"

That's honest and respectful.

Your honesty needs to be framed in a way that is respectful of your spouse's feelings. This is not to say that you shouldn't convey information they may not agree with or may upset them. It simply means that you package your delivery in a considerate and sensitive manner.

Often times, we are afraid to tell our mate that they have offended us in some way. When we don't address strong, negative feelings about our spouse's behavior, resentment and bitterness begin to grow in our hearts and slowly we begin to change the way we treat our spouse. When we fail to bring a troublesome behavior to our spouses' attention, we also deprive them of the ability to openly discuss the behavior, accept their responsibility and make the necessary adjustments.

Honesty is the bedrock of marriage. It is essential for trust, for building compatibility, for creating a way of life that you both enjoy, and for maintaining the feelings of love in marriage. The fear of sharing information, thoughts, and feelings that your spouse may disagree with is often the result of a lack of trust and feeling safe. If you have been withholding very difficult information from your spouse, you might want to consider obtaining the help of a skilled professional to ease the process and assist both of you to heal from the damage in your relationship. Sharing with the assistance of a trained and caring third party can help facilitate this process and aid in the restoration of your relationship.

For millennia, words have eluded the very best poets and philosophers in their quest to analyze love, quantify love, explain love, or define love. But where words leave the brain numb, the heart knows when it sees love in action.

We have looked at some of the core behaviors of *married love*: patience, kind words, kind touch, humility, respect and honesty. These drive the many caring deeds of *married love*. When you practice these behaviors on a regular basis, you and your spouse will consistently experience the feelings of loving and being loved. You will ignite intimacy and romance in your marriage.

 *Coachable Moment*

1 How well do you handle your spouse's honesty? Do you become upset, yell, threaten, or criticize when your partner shares difficult information? When your spouse is transparent about their behaviors, what they need from you is a large dose of empathy. Your empathy will serve to open their heart to your response of their candor.

2 You would be well advised to make a practice of thanking your spouse for whatever information they share. If it is too difficult at the time for you to handle the things your spouse is sharing, then express your appreciation and ask for time to process what you've heard. Be sure to get back with your spouse and continue the discussion at an appropriate time.

3 When you share information with your partner, do it in a way that is calm and respectful. You may need to write down what you want to say and go over it before you deliver it orally to your spouse.

Maturity begins to grow when you can sense your concern for others outweighing your concern for yourself.
– John MacNaughton

Suggested Reading:

His Needs, Her Needs: Building an Affair-Proof Marriage, Willard F. Harley, Jr. Grand Rapids, MI: Revell, 2011.

The Five Love Languages: the Secret to Love that Lasts, Gary Chapman. Chicago: Northfield Publishing, 2010.

Sexual Chemistry

"Sex is more than an act of pleasure, it's the ability to be able to feel so close to a person, so connected, so comfortable that it's almost breathtaking to the point you feel you can't take it. And at this moment you're a part of them."

– Author Unknown

Awkward Is Natural; Awesome Is Learned

Carrie and Sam had dreamed of this moment since they first met. Their wedding night had finally arrived. This was it, the moment they would consummate everything. She was looking for romantic passion, he for the ultimate physical climax. However, they found it was … awkward.

In the movies and on TV, sex is portrayed as easy; never clumsy or uncomfortable. People are just born great lovers. Virtually every sexual encounter is a mountaintop moment. There are no sexual diseases among beautiful people, and somehow we buy into the fantasy that if we will just get naked, magical things will happen.

Owning a bicycle doesn't make you Lance Armstrong any more than owning a spaceship makes you Neil Armstrong. Being in a relationship doesn't make you a great lover, although our culture would suggest that if you're not a great lover, there's something seriously wrong with you.

There are those in our culture that would suggest great sex is merely physical and therefore, those who enjoy it most are the population's most athletic people. The rest of us athletically – challenged individuals should just go read a book or watch reruns on TV.

They overlook one important fact – that's not the way it works! Mutually fulfilling sex is not as easy as most think it should be.

To become a great lover, to create passionate pleasure that captivates body, mind, and emotion requires knowledge and experience. Without it, sex is too often synonymous with frustration and disappointment. Great sex is the culmination of consistently practicing the behaviors of *married love*. Exciting sexual chemistry is a celebration of the emotional health of your daily relationship.

Challenges to Sexual Pleasure

So what gets in the way of your married sexual pleasure?

> *Our pre-schoolers get in through the locked door asking
>   if they can wrestle, too …*
> *Hamburgers with onions for dinner …*
> *That leaking toilet …*
> *The late movie is especially good tonight …*
> *I heard a noise …*

So much for the unscientific data. Now let's look at some actual data.

There are many issues that cause challenges to your sexual pleasure. Some of the most common causes for sexual issues in marriage are:

> *Distorted cultural and religious perspectives about sex*
> *Lack of knowledge regarding you and your mate's sexuality*
> *The inability to talk about sexual pleasure with your spouse*
> *Demanding schedules (jobs and children) rob you of energy*
> *Sexual abuse as a child or adult*
> *Infidelity on the part of one or both spouses*

We live in a sex-saturated culture and it is assumed that everyone knows a lot about sex. However, just because everybody is talking about sex doesn't mean they actually know what they are talking about. It's kind of like politics.

Knowing What's Sexy

One of the cultural distortions regarding sex involves a fixation on the physical. And the amazing thing is this varies as time passes. In some eras, women were only sexy if they were very thin. Men were only sexy if they had hair on their chests.

Later, women were only sexy if they had large breasts and men were only sexy if they shaved the hair off of their chests.

So what changed?

Our perceptions as driven by our culture and our media.

And no matter the trend of "what's sexy," we're bombarded with unrealistic images of perfect bodies. Usually these incredible physical specimens are attributed to some kind of diet or something concocted with Photoshop.

I see many couples whose ability to enjoy sex is damaged by these distortions: men who worry about "shrinkage," wives who are uncomfortable being naked with the lights on. They are concerned their breasts aren't large enough and the rest of their body is ... well, too large.

The reality is, if only people with perfect bodies were qualified to have great sex, the population would be considerably less – by say, several hundred billion.

To have healthy and pleasurable sex, you need to be comfortable with and able to enjoy your lover's body as well as your own. Don't compare yourself to images that have been airbrushed and color-corrected in order to sell you retail products or tickets to the cinema. Remember that sex is a physical expression of loving the one that you value most.

I've worked with couples whose bodies are far from cultural perfection and yet, they enjoy a great, pleasurable sex life.

Shelly said this about her husband, "It helps that my husband finds me sexy in anything. I've gained some weight and when I get down about it he makes sweet comments or pats my butt to let me know he loves me unconditionally. That alone makes me want him more each day."

God Created Sex; Satan Created Snickering

Before the fall, the Bible tells us Adam and Eve were naked and innocent. Somehow, I doubt they spent their days just playing checkers and eating apples. Sex was most probably an incredible, beautiful, intense, loving physical experience. Talk about paradise! Of course, the serpent showed up and helped them figure out that they were naked. Shame, guilt, maybe even snickering at how funny they looked to each other followed, and we've all been struggling with our self-image ever since.

God not only created us male and female, but he designed a special, unique mating relationship. "A man shall leave his father and mother and be joined to his wife, and they shall become one flesh. And they were not ashamed" (Genesis 2:24,25). God's original one-flesh companionship gives us wonderful insights into the kind of relationship He intended for us.

The Bible assumes sexual activity in marriage. It is endorsed and made beautiful. It becomes something ugly when we allow cultural distortions to degrade the beauty and power of sex. That's usually when the snickering begins.

Unfortunately, many times our confused understandings about sex cause us to react to distortions with more distortions.

Sex for Pleasure

It's okay for our *married love* sexual experiences to be pleasurable.

Solomon was history's wisest man, and in the Song of Solomon, you'll experience beautiful, poetic prose that celebrates sexual, *married love*.

Listen to these words: "How beautiful you are and how pleasing, O love, with your delights! Your stature is like that of the palm and your breasts like clusters of fruit. I said, 'I will climb the palm tree; I will take hold of its fruit.' May your breasts be like the clusters of the vine, the fragrance of your breath like apples and your mouth like the best wine" (Song of Solomon 7:6-9).

Consider your spouse for a moment. Husbands, have you really invested such a large part of your life just pursuing a pair of perfect breasts? Wives, have you studied the ultimate masculine physique? Could it possibly be that what you *value* goes deeper?

> *Her little, feminine laugh that you've always found so cute?*
> *That look he gives you that communicates more than any*
>   *words he could utter?*
> *The way you hold each other when you just need comfort?*

The Bible uses a brilliant term to describe intimacy between married couples – it says they *know* each other: "And the man knew Eve his wife; and she conceived ...." (English Standard Version)

There's a powerful message in the word *know*. The message is that the intimacy between a husband and wife allows them to understand – *to know* –themselves and their spouse in a complex physical, emotional, and spiritual way.

Married Love

Sex in *married love* is about each partner looking to satisfy their spouse as well as themselves. The spiritual component of *married love*, the understanding of the *value* of your mate, makes sex incredible.

"So why isn't our sex incredible?"

Just as it is with accomplishing anything worthwhile, it takes work, experience, knowledge, and some patience.

But I promise you, it *is* worth it.

Talking About Sex Is Essential

As a result of the cultural distortions we've already mentioned, I often see couples that are uncomfortable talking about their sexual needs with each other.

Spouses don't come with instructions as to what gives them sexual pleasure, so you're going to have to talk about it.

You need to be open with each other and talk about your preferences, what you enjoy, what you would like to explore, and what you are uncertain about. When you are comfortable talking about sexuality, it can open you up to getting correct information and exploring new ways to enjoy the mutual pleasures of sex.

Script for the Sex Talk

Emotions are often intense during sex talks because of frustrations over sexual performance. When talking about sex, avoid reacting to your spouse with attacking and blaming words.

Suppose you are a woman who has rarely been able to experience a pleasurable sexual response, and you are trying to tell your husband at what point in the experience of sexual intercourse your feelings of excitement get turned off.

"Well if you didn't always _____
_____ *."*

To him, that just sounds like you believe it's all his fault. He may get defensive and the communication degrades into an unproductive argument.

Try it this way:

"What seems to happen to me is I am enjoying you and feeling turned on – but then I start to get anxious when _____
_____ *happens and that seems to be it for me."*

Do you want to add some variety to your sexual experience? Utilize the five sex-talk guidelines that are listed below in the *Coachable Moment*. One way to introduce the subject of sexual variety is to ask:

> *What are your thoughts about (name something related to*
> *sexual variety that you've been thinking about)?*

The discussion must be respectful with a balance of listening and speaking so you can understand your spouse's thoughts and feelings. The purpose of the dialogue is to plant the seed; not to experiment with something new right then, unless both are willing.

Moving past personal sexual boundaries takes time. Move slowly here. Husbands have a tendency to want to rush things and this almost always leads to trouble in the bedroom. This discussion works best in a sex talk away from the bedroom. Sexual experimentation and variety are important, and must be handled with sensitive patience, but it pays exciting and pleasurable dividends!

 *Coachable Moment*

Here is a simple format to follow when talking about sex. The dialogue must be sensitive, considerate, and respectful, with a balance of listening and speaking.

1 Spouse number one shares their feelings about sex.

2 Spouse number two listens and then summarizes what he/she has understood that spouse number one is saying and feeling. "Here is what I hear you saying ..."

3 Spouse number one then confirms, clarifies or expands on the summary made by partner number two.

4 The discussion continues until spouse number one is satisfied that spouse number two understands their sexual needs and is willing to honor their request.

5 When you're talking about sex, be real! Being phony just to be able to say something good about your partner doesn't help. The phoniness can invariably be detected and breaks down trust in the relationship. Being honest does not mean being insensitive to your spouse, but that what you do say is an accurate statement of what you feel.

Sex: It's More Than the Big "O"

"Sex lies at the root of life, and we can never learn to reverence life until we know how to understand sex."
– HENRY ELLIS

In Woody Allen's 1973 movie *Sleeper*, his character, Miles Monroe, awakes in the year 2173 to find that sex is now accomplished in a small booth called the *Orgasmatron*, which brings ultimate sexual pleasure quickly and efficiently. Allen's character is appalled – as should we be.

The *Orgasmatron* is a disturbing metaphor for removing human emotion and spirituality from sex. It reduces sex to a self-centered physical experience. In *married love*, sex is about each partner looking to satisfy their spouse as well as themselves. The spiritual component of *married love*, valuing and honoring your mate, makes sex incredible. Essential to having a passionate, off-the-charts sexual experience, is understanding your spouse's unique sexual design.

That Venus And Mars Thing

Many of us just don't understand the differences between men and women and how those differences impact their sexual relationship.

Kim verbalized this disparity: "Jerry and I need help with our sex life. He wants sex every day. For me, once a week would be plenty, so we get frustrated with one another. Jerry thinks something's wrong with me and I think the same thoughts about him. Sex is actually driving a wedge between us."

Husbands think their wives are unresponsive and wives think their husbands are obsessed with sex.

So what is normal when it comes to *married love* sex? How do you get to that point at which you can meet at a comfortable place that meets both your needs?

Maybe it's like taking a trip – perhaps you should consult a map.

Reading Intimacy Maps to Get Where You Want to Go

The key to dealing with our differences gets back to our intimacy maps in the area of sexuality. Problems develop in a couples' sex life because the husband tries to love his wife according to his intimacy map and she loves him using hers. Many times, they end up using very different routes to get to where they want to go. When that happens, problems develop because neither spouse feels the love the other intends to give during the journey.

So what are the critical differences?

Men view sex in a compartmentalized way, just as they often tend to view work, recreation and family as separate entities. A husband can have a horrible day at work, his car breaks down on the way home and he can still get in the mood immediately. Sex, just like his favorite meal, makes him feel better.

A woman's sex drive is impacted by everything that happens in her day. Foreplay and arousal is just one aspect that affects your wife's sex drive. Instead of being compartmentalized, she views sex as interrelated with all her experiences. What happens in one part of her network sets off a chain reaction that impacts all others.

If your wife has had a tough day at work or with the kids, or you've had an argument, a chain reaction is released that impacts her sexual desire. This is why she may say something like, "It's been a tough day and I have a headache. I'm not in the mood for sex."

Another major difference between men and women is the length of time between arousal and sex. A man enjoys sex more like a sprint. Testosterone, one of the hormones responsible for sex drive, is 20 - 40% higher in men than women. This causes your husband's natural, sexual arousal to happen very quickly.

A woman experiences sex more like a marathon – an enduring, pleasurable experience that's like a soothing, warm bath. The guy can't wait to get there, but his wife wants to enjoy the journey.

Guys: Read Your Wife's Intimacy Map

– Don't Take Shortcuts

You need to be sensitive to what is going on in your wife's life. Be aware that everything leading up to sex is impacting her experience. Wives' sexual urges are the delicate combination of biology, temperament, surroundings, and a sense of how connected she is to you. Women assimilate everything that is occurring in their immediate environment and are sexually aroused when they have time, energy, and romance to turn them on.

Your wife was designed by God with a need to emotionally relate, so in most cases, your wife is aroused only after she feels emotionally close to you. If you are not aware of the need or you haughtily dismiss it, she may feel that you are only using her as an object to selfishly satisfy your sexual desire.

 *Coachable Moment*

Husbands, when you are aware of your wife's intimacy map and when you become sensitive to it, she will be able to open up, becoming free in experimenting and expressing her sexuality. Here are five suggestions:

1 First, converse!

One way that emotional connection is made with a wife is through considerate conversation. Your wife does much of her thinking out loud – she processes her thoughts and emotions through talking. The message your wife needs to receive from you is, *"You are the love of my life. I want to understand what you are saying and how you are feeling."* When considerate conversation becomes the norm in your relationship, you will find your wife more responsive. For your wife, talking opens the door to emotional connection, intimacy, arousal, and sexual desire.

2 Help with the kids.

Assisting with your children is another way you create sexual connection with your wife. She needs to feel that you are involved with rearing the kids. Stay at home with the kids and send her off on a ladies night out. This will pay big dividends for you later.

3 Share the load.

Sharing the responsibilities of household chores is also emotionally important to your wife. After she has prepared a big meal, send her to the den while you clean up the kitchen. Do more around the house than just take out the garbage.

4 Focus on the journey, not just the destination.

During sex, don't focus exclusively on the orgasm finish line. Slow down and take more time. Your wife is not your personal *Orgasmatron*. Focus on enjoying the journey, not just reaching the destination. Take some time to surprise your wife. Light candles, put on some romantic music, and give her a nonsexual massage. You might even go that extra mile and write or read poetry to her! When you have the sex talk we mentioned above, you will then know her sexual intimacy map and the behaviors that she enjoys.

5 Unwind slowly.

After orgasm, a man is finished and can roll over and go to sleep or get up and go about his business. A woman though, is very different. She has a slower unwinding time emotionally. It's important for you to snuggle with your wife, holding her tenderly afterwards. One of the major complaints I hear from wives is that they feel used by their husbands when they don't take the time to help her feel valued and honored during the afterglow of sex.

Wives: Read Your Husband's Intimacy Map
– Don't Make Him Keep His Stallion In The Stable

As guys, you need to understand that our testosterone is high velocity fuel. Your husband probably likes adventure movies, fast cars, football, athletic competition, and falls asleep during chick flicks. Although he may not put it into words, his approach to sex is probably like that as well – picture a wild stallion running at full speed through a spectacular meadow.

At least part of this great, adventurous spirit may have been attractive to you when you were dating.

But now you're married.

Marriage brings different responsibilities and feelings. Wives may change their personal habits to meet those responsibilities. And when their husbands continue to want their sexual encounters to remain the same, it's not uncommon for women to think these guys are just untamable sexual beasts.

Much of your husband's need for sexual release is based on physical, hormonal needs. Many studies agree that because of sperm production – natural testosterone – men, on average, want sexual release every seventy-two hours, or three days. This is on average, and younger men often need it daily or even multiple times a day.

Your husband needs sex frequently.

It's how guys are physically and emotionally wired. One study suggests no less than 50% and up to as high as 90% of a husband's self-image – his feeling like a man – is locked up in his sexuality.

In addition, a great deal of your husband's emotional fulfillment occurs during sex. While he is at work he is focused on job-related objectives that cater to his cognitive side. Emotions usually play a small part in his workday. Sex is a significant way for him to connect with his feelings. It opens him up to receive your love and to give his love to you. Even if a man is stressed from the day, if his wife is feeling loved, supported and enjoys sex with him, he can be immediately rejuvenated. Although it seems as if sex makes him feel better, it is really that he is simply feeling again and is able to accept his wife's love.

Studies find that it is difficult for the man to experience sexual gratification unless his wife also finds sexual contentment. When both husband and wife join in the sexual experience, they both find physical and emotional fulfillment. Many men complain their wives just lay there, waiting for it to be over.

Married love gives our mates something that may not be the primary way we need to feel loved. Because you love your husband, you love him the way he needs to be loved.

Most wives I counsel do not realize how much their husband's identity is tied in to their sexuality. For a guy, sex means more than just a physical act. When a man feels their wife desires them sexually, it has a profound effect on other areas of their lives. It gives them an increasing sense of confidence and well-being that carries over into every other aspect of their lives.

The flipside of this coin also carries a profoundly negative effect. When a husband feels rejected sexually, he not only feels rejected in a physical aspect, but also that his wife is somehow rejecting him as a man.

A wild stallion never let out of a stall will become miserable. This is why you need to make sex a priority in your marriage.

 *Coachable Moment*

Wives, by understanding your husband's intimacy map and what his intimacy fuel is, you will know what turns him. Here are three ways on how to connect:

1 **Make an advance.**

Do you remember the early part of your relationship? Pat him on the backside; tell him he looks sexy and that he turns you on. Flirt with him. Your husband will probably enjoy being approached by you first. Your advances will make him feel attractive. Your husband doesn't always need to be the one to initiate sex.

2 **Be willing to experiment.**

Ask your husband what gives him sexual pleasure. There may be things he would like to explore that make you uncertain. Take time to talk about these areas. Read, learn, and talk about sex as we mentioned earlier. Don't just talk about what you don't like, but also what he does that turns you on. Let sex become an exciting and dynamic adventure.

3 **Be creative.**

Even though guys tend to be more physically oriented, they also have an emotional side. From time to time, set a romantic mood for your husband. By understanding his intimacy map and intimacy fuel, you will know what turns him on. Then surprise him.

Darla said, "I surprised my husband with a shower together. It's something we have to do anyway, so we do it together. Once our daughter's down for the night, we both hop into a steamy shower and talk about whatever's on our minds. Our troubles and fears go 'down the drain' and it lets us slow down, relax, and enjoy each other."

Even if you're not in the mood, you can jumpstart your sex drive by just getting started. Act your way into the feelings and desire. Since men are more prone to visual stimulation and instant gratification, turn him on while he watches you slip into something sexy.

Three Types Of Sex

In helping couples meet one another's sexual needs, I teach them that there are three types of sex.

1 Fast Food Sex

You 've been busy working and haven't had a chance to eat since breakfast. It is 2:00, your stomach is growling, and you're starved. You take a break from work and run to the nearest fast food place for something to eat. Now you're satisfied and can concentrate on your work.

Wives, *fast food sex* is especially important to your husband. We noted that due to men's hormones, they have a biological need for sex more frequently than you do. Testosterone and semen build up and the pressure is on for release. Some call this the need for "a quickie." This sends the message to your husband, "I understand your intimacy map and your intimacy fuel. I love you."

2 Romantic Sex

Okay husbands, now it's your turn. Plan a special evening for your wife (or morning, depending on your schedule). If you have preschool children, make arrangements for a sitter, or put the kids to bed early. Do whatever it takes for you and your spouse to be alone. Light the bedroom with candles, have romantic music playing, put rose petals on the bed in the shape of a heart or give her a massage (stay away from the genitals and breast until invited).

These are just a few suggestions, but you get the point. When you and your wife talk about sex, you will know what she likes and you will be able to give it to her. Going to this effort sends the message to your wife, "You're my queen. I'm here to serve your needs. Let this evening be all about your pleasure. Relax and enjoy … I love you."

3 Fun and Games Sex

It is easy to get into a rut. Hurried sex, the same positions, the same place. Plan an exciting romp with some new ideas. Exploring fun and games gives you the opportunity to practice the five steps of having a sex talk.

Jennifer shared, "My husband and I both work full-time, and so we prefer to spend our free time with our child. Instead of hiring a babysitter at night or on the weekend, we leave work early and meet for a movie and dinner — or at home for a rendezvous. What's great about these daytime dates is that we have enough energy to really enjoy each other."

Brent confided: "We have secret 'afternoon delights' in my home office when our youngest is napping and our oldest is otherwise occupied (but within earshot) in another room. It's a great release for both of us, and we feel so naughty." Let your imagination run its course … you'll have some fun!

SCHEDULE SEX

As busy professionals with two children, my wife and I scheduled sex on a regular basis.

Your response is probably, *"Are you kidding? Scheduling sex sounds about as sexy as making your next dentist's appointment!"*

Let's face it, if it's not scheduled, sometimes sex can be the first thing that goes. So even if it doesn't feel very exciting at first, be patient and keep your appointments. If you don't feel in the mood on the day of your date, just relax and let it happen. Generate anticipation between the two of you for your sex appointments.

Actually, the excitement that can build when you have a set sex date can be pretty hot. Tease and titillate each other. Discuss some of the things you're planning to do for each other. Prepare for the date the way you did at the beginning of your relationship. Wear something special. Set the scene. Sex dates can foster a real sense of togetherness as they open the door to more romance and flirting and lessen the pressure to argue over differing expectations.

Here are some key points for you to remember:

1 Sex has a spiritual component, honoring and valuing your spouse as the number one person in your life.

2 Men and women are not wired the same sexually.

3 The primary sex organ is the brain, not the penis or clitoris. Sexiness is in our minds and attitudes, not our body shape and size.

4 Sex is subject to inertia — erotic passion must be kept in motion.

5 The backbone of a great sex life is a commitment to value and honor your spouse in the little daily stuff of life.

6 Busy couples often have to schedule sex. This doesn't remove the exciting spontaneity that can occur in the moment.

 *Coachable Moment*

1 Name a fresh insight you've learned about male/female sexual differences.

2 Have a sex talk and share your new insights about sex.

3 Discuss how you are going to implement these new findings in your marriage.

4 Share which one of the three types of sex is your favorite and the reason.

5 Not having enough sex because of a busy schedule? Take out your calendar and schedule sex!

Suggested Reading:

Read through the Song of Solomon. Use a traditional version of the Bible (such as the *New International Version*) along with a paraphrase (such as *The Message*). Take turns reading a chapter at a time.

The Gift of Sex: A Guide to Sexual Fulfillment, Clifford and Joyce Penner. Nashville: W Publishing Group, 2003.

A Celebration of Sex: A Guide to Enjoying God's Gift of Sexual Intimacy, Douglas E. Rosenau. Nashville: Thomas Nelson, Inc., 2002.

Romance and Intimacy: Keeping the Flame in Your Marriage

"Love and magic have a great deal in common.
They enrich the soul, delight the heart.
And they both take practice."
– Nora Roberts

A football player for a Big 12 college was describing his recruitment process:

"When they were recruiting me, all the coaches were really nice. And then after I got there, they all suddenly turned really mean. They started yelling at me all the time."

That's kind of like marriage. We buy into the myth that we only need romance in order to attract that future spouse. Once we have them, that becomes job is done and we don't need to keep getting what we already have.

But really, we do.

Romance and intimacy are closely related and tie all of the steps of *married love* together: forgiveness, a servant's heart, commitment to the behaviors of love, connectedness as friends, and sexual chemistry. Let's look at how romance and intimacy can keep enchantment in your marriage.

Romance

Romance is an atmosphere where you feel unconditional love, value, and appreciation. Romance is an intense, positive emotion that bonds you to your spouse. Women intuitively know what romance is.

Most guys need some training.

Romantic love is an emotion created at least partially as a result of the way you're treated. This is the same dynamic we found in our section on *Agape Love.* Caring love is treating your spouse in a way that shows you understand their intimacy map and their intimacy fuel.

Some people think that romance is easy, that anybody can be romantic with very little work. After all, it works that way in the movies.

That movie scene probably had a crew of more than fifty people, working for days to set the mood for the camera. And if they didn't get it right the first time, they would just redo everything again and again until they did.

The truth is, it isn't easy – but with some work, you can do it.

Romance is not Event Planning

First begin by thinking of romance not as an event, but as a day-to-day relationship, a friendship with your spouse that continues to grow. It's asking each other about their day, how a hobby or special project is going, or even just reminiscing together. It's sharing common interests and just taking the time to enjoy each other's company.

It's a joint process.

Many times a spouse will try to initiate romance with a surprise dinner or an unexpected vacation they planned. But then they are disappointed when the event isn't the dream date or getaway they had imagined. It's not that the recipient isn't appreciative of the effort, but what is fun or relaxing for one person may not be for the other.

"She bought me one of those European man-purses – along with tickets to the football game!"

"He showed up on a new Harley he bought with a black helmet for me that had flames ... FLAMES! Then he announced we were going to Big Bend together – I've never even camped out!"

Since you aren't a mind reader, the only way to really know for sure what will impress your spouse is to ask.

"What is romantic to you?"

What is your idea of a dream date – where would you go, how dressed up would you want to be, what kind of restaurant? What kind of vacation would you want to go on – what time of year, where, what kind of hotel, what kind of activities?

Does your wife love art? Take her to a museum or an art fair.

Is your husband into the outdoors? Take a hike through the park or go fishing together.

For Erica and Kevin this meant a fishing trip. For Pat and Cathy, tickets to a musical theater. And for Jeff and Rita it was a weekend of college football.

Find out what your common interests are and build on them.

When you have your quarterly question/discussions time and learn your spouse's intimacy map and fuel, you will know exactly what they need.

It's also surprises.

Finding out what your spouse thinks is romantic doesn't mean that you still can't have surprises. It just may not be an unexpected date or weekend trip. It could be something simple like a note in a briefcase, a favorite meal or dessert, or offering to take your spouse to that new movie they've wanted to see.

It's consistency.

Romance isn't an event. It's not putting effort into planning a nice Friday night date when you've neglected your spouse the rest of the week.

It takes a consistent, intentional effort. But unless you're very creative, it may get harder and harder to think of new ways to keep the romance alive. So build up some resources to help you think of ideas. There are some good books on romantic date ideas. Start by asking your spouse what they enjoy. Do something once a day, once a week, once a month and something special once a year to let your spouse know that they're loved.

It's attention.

Focus on each other, not just on what you're doing together. Going to the park for the day? Don't take the briefcase or cell phone. Thinking of giving your wife flowers? Don't wait until you need to ask for a favor. Did your wife ask for a quiet stroll on the beach? Leave the fishing pole at home. Eliminate the distracters and focus on enjoying your time with each other.

By consistently practicing romance, you will have a continual, fulfilling relationship where you will have fun discovering each other.

Keep the friendship in your marriage relationship strong, plan events centered on shared interests, surprise each other with special tokens of love and give your spouse your undivided attention during your romantic times together.

Building a romantic atmosphere in your marriage won't happen overnight or without continual effort. Sometimes it takes a few romantic encounters to begin to get it right.

You may have hurt your spouse. Your spouse may have hurt you. As a result, you or your spouse may question the motives behind these nice gestures. Don't. Let it go. Let yourself believe these moments are real – just as you did when you were first dating.

That's how you find your way back to intimacy.

Intimacy

"What do you think the word *intimacy* means?"

This was the question I asked at a couples retreat. One woman responded with a play on the word.

"It's looking into me and seeing what's there."

She clarified the statement with: *"Intimacy is seeing into each other's life. It's knowing each other's strengths and weaknesses. It's being aware of each other's fears, hopes, and dreams."*

It was so cool – like she had been reading part one of this chapter.

Emotional intimacy isn't easy. It's making yourself known to your spouse by trusting them enough to verbally reveal personal information. Deep emotional intimacy is when we feel wholly accepted, respected and admired in the eyes of our spouse – even when they know our innermost fears, struggle, failures, hopes and dreams. Emotional intimacy fosters compassion and support, providing the firm foundation for a marriage to last a lifetime.

Too many marriages today try to exist without emotional intimacy. Because you and your spouse are always experiencing new things, you are both constantly changing.

So is your relationship.

When you don't share your current feelings with your spouse, he or she can't share your life. If you want to be understood, you need to help your spouse understand you. Over time, a marriage lacking intimacy will become empty and lifeless. Then the husband and wife will slowly drift apart.

Emotional intimacy is the glue that holds relationships together, yet it's a challenge for many couples to experience.

Challenges to Developing Emotional Intimacy

Why is it so hard to develop emotional intimacy?

First, there's the fear of rejection.

> *"If I share the essence of who I really am, you might criticize, reject, or judge the real me."*

Second, there's unfamiliarity with our own feelings, needs, or wants.

> *"If I'm not sure what I feel or need, how can I share it with you?"*

Third, there's a lack of vocabulary to communicate our feelings accurately, or to verbalize exactly what we want or need.

> *"If I don't know the words to describe what I'm feeling or needing, then it's easier to just keep my thoughts to myself. I don't want to sound stupid."*

Fourth, we expect our spouse to just know.

> *"If you really loved me, you would know!"*

We are not mind readers. You're going to have to openly share yourself – and trust your spouse to do the same.

Coachable Moment

There are many ways to weave romance and intimacy into your daily relationship. Use these suggestions as a romance/intimacy assessment. Put a check mark by the ones you currently practice and an "X" by the ones you don't. For a reality check, let your spouse look over the list. Now, develop a plan to integrate the ones with an "X" into your daily relationship.

1 **Pay attention to your own emotions.**

   Many of us have two words to describe our emotions: happy or angry. But there are dozens of emotions that fall in between those words. Become familiar with your emotions. Pay attention to what really goes on inside of you. You might even want to keep a journal of your thoughts and emotions throughout the day.

2 **Become familiar with your inner self.**

   What are the messages that run in your mind throughout the day? Where do you feel you don't measure up and, as a result, you fear being vulnerable?

3 **How has your hurried pace of life impacted your relationship?**

   Has this hurried pace been a false place of safety for you to keep an emotional distance from your spouse? Is your excuse that there just isn't time to share?

4 **Evaluate your past.**

Take a mental walk back to your childhood and consider the emotional connectedness of the family you grew up in. Was it okay to express feelings in your home? Did your family really know one another or were they simply operating as roommates living under one roof?

5 **Commit to become a *safe* person for your spouse to share emotions, thoughts, and feelings.**

If you criticize or try to fix your spouse when they share their feelings, you will close their door to intimacy.

6 **Increase the time you spend together as a couple.**

Intimacy can't be created without spending time talking. Don't make it just about the events of the day, but also talk about how you feel about the events of the day.

7 **Deal with conflict swiftly.**

Don't resort to the silent treatment or snide remarks. Learn to get the issue out on the table and treat your spouse with respect when you disagree. This will grow trust and deepen intimacy.

8 **Strive for open communication, the ability to discuss anything with your spouse.**

Open communication includes the sincere expression of thoughts and feelings as well as careful listening. Signs of poor communication include: feeling reluctant to tell your spouse about the events of your day; being unwilling to listen when your spouse is explaining how they feel; or discrediting your spouse's feelings with words like, "You shouldn't feel that way!"

9 Sincere apologies can work wonders.

Recognizing mistakes, taking responsibility for them, expressing remorse for any hurt caused, and making a commitment to change the hurtful behavior are all essential to mending the relationship after a mistake.

For spouses who have created a chasm of hurts that separate them, offering a sincere and humble apology is the first step in building a bridge over that chasm. Even if you believe your partner made the mistake, you can begin the healing by finding something you did that calls for an apology.

10 Practice forgiveness.

This is the process of letting go of anger, the desire for revenge, and obsessively thinking about the times your spouse has hurt you. It includes giving your spouse permission to have weaknesses, make mistakes, and change. Seeing the goodness and strengths of your spouse –along with the weaknesses – can open up emotional space for goodwill to build toward your spouse.

Forgiveness does not automatically create trust or reconciliation, nor does it mean you approve of bad behavior. Forgiveness is an important early step toward rebuilding a fractured relationship. In Chapter Four, we established the absolute necessity of a forgiving spirit in practicing the behaviors of *married love*. This may be an fitting time to review it.

11 Apply appropriate boundaries.

These are the limits you place on your relationship. The limits can be created individually or as a couple. These limits include saying "no" when your spouse asks you to do something that goes against your values, or is more than you can handle. By setting firm, clear boundaries for yourself and respecting the boundaries of your partner, you create the feelings of safety and trust.

Romance and intimacy are related. They come as a result of your intentional, disciplined effort to demonstrate caring deeds to your spouse. When romance and intimacy are a part of your daily relationship, romance, intimacy, and sex will be a joyous and pleasurable celebration of the emotional and spiritual health of your marriage.

What is being in love?
Joy, Creative playfulness that pushes limits
Contentment, the ability to savor the moment
To be thrilled to be where you are and
appreciate the present.
– DAVID FOX, M.D.

Suggested Reading:

Becoming Soul Mates: Cultivating Spiritual Intimacy in the Early Years of Marriage, Les and Leslie Parrott. Grand Rapids, Michigan: Zondervan, 1995.

The Question That
Can Save Your Marriage

*"Successful people ask better questions,
and as a result, they get better answers."*
– Tony Robins

*T*he question is designed to keep the fires of passion ignited in your marriage by staying current with you and your spouse's personal relational needs:

How do you fall out of love?

"My spouse has changed ... and it's not good."

Origins of unhappy marriages can be traced back to a failure to understand and consistently practice the behaviors that a spouse needs from their partner in order to have the feelings of being loved.

The only way you can have an intimate connection is to know your spouse's unique intimacy needs. You should consistently and intentionally provide the behaviors that will meet their needs.

But how do you know what your spouse needs to feel loved? Studies have revealed in a general way what men and women need in a marriage to feel loved. However, none address the specific and unique behaviors your husband or wife specifically needs from you to feel loved.

In fact, the specifics frequently change on a regular basis.

So how do you know what you spouse needs you to do to have the *feelings* of love?

You ask *The Question*.

The Question

Here's how *the question* works.

Get alone with one another. Allow approximately 45 to 60 minutes for the discussion and then ask your spouse: *"What do I need to be doing so that you feel loved?"*

When your spouse asks you this question, your response should be framed with:

"To feel loved by you, I need _____.*"*
Then tell your spouse what behaviors you need from them.

My wife and I ask *the question* once a quarter. By being intentional in asking *the question*, we have avoided drifting apart over the forty-three years of our marriage. Another benefit of a quarterly question is that you get your needs out in the open. You talk about them, you can manage them, and they are quickly repaired.

In our last quarterly question discussion, my wife said that she needed me to, "… keep the kitchen countertop picked up and clean."

I asked her to tell me at least once a week how much she appreciated my work.

Two simple requests, easily done, without harsh words or hurt feelings. In fact, our feelings for being loved were met and we were drawn closer together. These two behaviors are simple, but specific caring deeds that communicate, "I love you!"

One of the by-products of having quarterly discussions is that when you ask *the question*, the response is often, "I don't need anything … just keep doing what you are doing." This in itself provides solid affirmation that things are going well in your marriage.

Erica tells how her husband meets her intimacy and relational needs: *"He takes good care of me. When we go to bed at night he always makes sure that we're touching in some way or he will cuddle with me. He does simple things like cooking or going to the grocery store, or making sure that we have a fire in the fireplace so I'm not cold. He makes it a point to tend to my needs."*

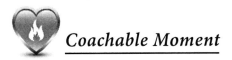 *Coachable Moment*

Here's the structure for having *The Question* discussion:

1 First, your request must be positive.

A positive request aims for initiating or increasing caring behaviors, not a decrease in unwanted responses. It sends the message, "This is what I need you do." For example, you might say, "I need you to help me with the kids at the end of the day;" instead of "You never help me with the kids."

Or, "I would like for you to pick up my clothes from the cleaners each Wednesday," rather than, "You never do anything for me," or a sharp, "Pick up my clothes on Wednesday!"

Granted, there will often be annoying or disrespectful behaviors that you want your spouse to stop. This is where you will have to think through what you are going to request.

It's critical to develop a gentle spirit and the internal strength to control your words so they don't come across as sarcastic or demanding. The tone of the question discussion must be respectful, or it loses it power to change behavior. Be careful that you don't turn this into a way to manipulate your spouse.

2 **Your request must be specific.**

In coaching sessions, I often hear spouses make general statements like, "I just need you to show me that you love me!" I'll respond, "Okay, so what specifically does your spouse need to do that would make you feel loved?" A specific response would be, "I would like for you to call me twice a day to check on how I'm doing."

Or instead of saying, "Show more consideration for me," you might say something like, "Please call if you are going to be late for dinner. That would let me know that you are concerned about my feelings."

To help in wording the questions, ask yourself: "What specific behavior do I need from my spouse in order to feel loved, honored, and valued?"

3 **The behaviors should be such that they can be done on a regular basis.**

When your marriage is in trouble and needs repair, the behaviors should be immediate and frequent. These actions build trust and indicate that you sincerely want to make lasting changes. High-rate responses at this stage are behaviors that can be done at least once daily.

Kelly shared how her husband consistently communicates and demonstrates his love: *"He does a lot of things for me. He is conscious of what I need, of what makes me happy. He tells me he loves me and just does simple things. When we are getting in the car, he opens the door. He holds my hand and continually gives me visible signs that he loves and honors me."*

The 3 x 5 Marriage-Saver

A skill I recommend to couples to help implement these behavior changes is what I call the *3 x 5 Reminders*. Take a 3 x 5 note card and write down your spouses' request. Place the card where you will see it daily to remind you of the new behavior. This helps to avoid what I call the "start up and fizzle" marriage derailer.

Your spouse asks you to start or stop a behavior. You begin the process, do it for a while, but then fall back into your old patterns of behavior. Your spouse assumes you weren't sincere – if you were, you would have continued the new behavior. When you "start-up and fizzle" several times, trust flies out the window. Your spouse takes any new pledges to change as hollow and manipulative.

Countless couples have ended up in my office, and eventually in the divorce courts, because of failed start-ups. I hear …

"I've asked you a thousand times to …"
"I just get busy and forget."
"I promise this time it'll be different."

"Yeah, it'll be different – How many times have I heard that!
It'll be 'different' for a couple of weeks and then back to
business as usual. I've had it with your lies and empty
promises."

It's at this point they end up in my office and a tearful "start-up and fizzle" spouse begs for another opportunity to make it right. However, by this time, it's virtually too late. When it gets to that point, if the marriage isn't all ready dead, it's severely comatose.

Avoid the *Start-Up and Fizzle*

Commit to Act
To avoid *start-up and fizzle* in your marriage, you must make a commitment to act on the daily behaviors irrespective of whether or not you spouse does.

Do not allow, wait and see thinking to derail your commitment to act. Never say to yourself, "I'll wait and see if my spouse does this, then I will, too." Draw on the power of a servant spirit to act as the motivation for you to go first.

It is at this point that you probably will have to counter the thought, "I don't feel like doing this, it's hypocritical to act without the right feelings." *Married love* is based on knowing and doing the right thing for your spouse, not on what you're feeling. By consistently doing the right thing, you will recognize the value in your spouse and your relationship. Your feelings will eventually align with your behaviors. When the behaviors aren't present, the feelings are never experienced.

Jerrod's marriage had grown sour after eighteen years. When I asked him how he knew it was over, he said, "When she stopped putting my slippers by the bed each night." He went ahead to explain that when he and his wife were first married, they had a ritual of putting each other's slippers by the bed.

He lamented, "Somewhere along the line, we stopped doing that for each other and the marriage when downhill from there."

That, of course, is an oversimplification of why the marriage went wrong, but the little courtesies do count. They count a lot. As poet Edna St. Vincent Millay lamented, "Tis not love's going hurts my days, but that it went in little ways."

Small acts of kindness have great power because they demonstrate that you haven't taken your spouse for granted. You take time to listen to them, to consider their needs and act on them. They realize you value them and the relationship. "The roots of the deepest love," wrote philosopher Von Herder, "die in the heart if not tenderly cherished."

Say *Thank You*

When your spouse does the things you have requested to meet your intimacy needs, let them know that you notice and appreciate what they are doing. One group of social scientists discovered that the phrases "Shhh!" and "What's going on?" are more common in most homes than, "Thank you."

Saying "Thank you for caring" is a powerful way to inspire your spouse to continue the behaviors they began. Allen remarked, "My wife and I make it a habit to regularly communicate those things we admire or value in the other. This practice has strengthened our friendship." It's amazing how the little things done on a regular basis can keep you connected as friends.

Due to the negative energy built up over the years in your marriage, you may not have said, "thank you" to your spouse in a long time for anything they have done positive. But be careful.

At this point you can mentally discredit your spouse's actions by saying to yourself, *"You're just doing this because I asked you, so it's not really sincere."*

You're right!

They're doing it because you requested it. But, you are wrong in thinking it is not sincere. They may not feel like doing it, but they are doing it because they are allowing *agape love* instead of subjective feelings to motive them. Remember, it's not hypocritical to do what you know is right, even though you don't feel like doing it.

Caring deeds embody the needs of your spouse. When your spouse acts upon your request, focus on the fact that they want you to feel loved. They want to understand your unique needs and display the behaviors that meet those needs.

Most people don't feel understood by their spouse in a troubled marriage. Past hurts have formed a protective shell around a person's heart. As you demonstrate these new behaviors, be aware that you spouse may be skeptical. The way to disarm their skepticism is for your new behaviors to become relational habits that consistently feed the warmth that melts away the shell around your spouse's heart. As you develop the new habits of caring love, you will get to a place where your spouse feels your emotional presence in the behaviors. When that happens, you will have helped him or her see that you value the relationship and thus accept your motives as being genuine and sincere.

One of the greatest human needs is to feel understood. *Agape love* says, "I know you, I understand you, and I want to meet your unique relational needs." This creates the intimate connection of friendship and builds the foundation for *married love*.

Work-Life Balance

The Dash

I read of a man who stood to speak
At the funeral of a friend.
He referred to the dates on her tombstone
From the beginning to the end.
He noted that first came the date of birth
And spoke the following date with tears,
But he said what mattered most of all
Was the dash between those years.
For that dash represents all the time
That she spent alive on earth
And now only those who loved her
Know what that little line is worth.
For it matters not, how much we own;
The cars … the house … the cash,
What matters is how we live and love
And how we spend our dash.
So when your eulogy's being read
With your life's actions to rehash
Would you be proud of the things they say
About how you spent your dash?

– Linda Ellis

Making Married Love work takes discipline to manage your priorities in order that you can spend time together building a lasting, lifelong, intimate relationship.

Frank was Executive Vice President for a large banking company. His marriage was on the rocks. In our first discussion he made it clear: "Mike, my career at the bank is more important that my wife and kids." Frank chose to give up family vacations, Pee Wee Football, anniversary and birthday dinners, lunch hour, and daily "us" talk-time with his wife. Eventually a divorce was the price he was willing to pay for an upwardly mobile career.

Is that the price you are willing to pay for your career?

For your marriage to work, you must spend both quality and quantity time together. Finding work-life balance in today's frenetically paced work place is no simple task.

When asked, "Can you have it all?" leadership author, Tom Peters states in his book, *A Passion for Excellence*, "No. The price of excellence is time, energy, attention and focus, at the very same time that energy, attention and focus could have gone toward enjoying your daughter's soccer game."

Spend more time at work than at home, and you'll miss out on a rewarding personal life. Then again, when you face challenges in your personal life, concentrating on your job can be difficult. Climbing the career ladder and building a lasting marriage and family is not easy, but not impossible either.

Whether the problem is too much focus on work or too little, when your work life and your personal life are out of balance, stress — along with its harmful effects — is the result. Undue stress limits your ability to give your best and enjoy your work and personal life.

The Discovery Group, in a recent study of more than 50,000 employees from a variety of organizations, found that two out of every five employees are dissatisfied with the balance between their work and their personal lives.

According to psychologist Sidney Jourard, fully 85% of your happiness in life will come from your personal relationships. Your interactions and the time that you spend with the people you care about is a major source of the pleasure, enjoyment and satisfaction that you derive daily.

In coaching busy professionals, I often hear them say, "I made it to the top of the career ladder and when I got there, there was no one to left to celebrate my victory with. My success created a relational desert."

The quality of your work is impacted by the quality of your personal life. An unhappy personal life spills over into your work. Work was not designed to do for us what relationships provide.

Some of the drivers of a failed work/life balance are:

Poor priority setting
Overly ambitious
A worrier
Can't relax
Time away from work is not exciting
Time management
Too intense
Workaholic

Take some time to reflect on this list. Check the ones that you struggle with.

There's No One-Size-Fits-All Answer to Work-Life Balance

The reference book, *For Your Improvement*, gives the following characteristics of work/life balance:

Maintains a conscious balance (balance: equipoise between contrasting, opposing, or interacting elements) between work and personal life so that one does not dominate the other

Is not one-dimensional
Knows how to attend to both
Gets what he/she wants from both

The good news is that you can take control of your work-life balance. There's no perfect, one- size-fits-all answer to the key question of how to achieve balance in our lives. There are, however, a number of ideas and solutions that can help you evaluate your relationship to work and apply some specific strategies for striking a healthier balance.

These ideas often require changes and modifications in the way you think and use your time, but the price is well worth it. You will find that by reorganizing your life in little ways, you can create an existence that gives you the highest quality and quantity of satisfaction overall.

 Coachable Moment

The ancient Greeks had a well-known maxim: "Man, know thyself." Knowing yourself is the starting point for achieving the work-life balance that you desire. The following true/false checklist will help you "know thyself" as you work toward managing much needed balance.

1 I find myself spending more and more time on work-related projects.
  _____ True _____ False

2 I often feel I don't have any time for myself — or for my family and friends.
  _____ True _____ False

3 No matter what I do, it seems that every minute of every day is always scheduled for something.

_____ True _____ False

4 Sometimes I feel as though I've lost sight of who I am and why I chose this job/career.

_____ True _____ False

5 I can't remember the last time I was able to find the time to take a day off to do something fun — something just for me.

_____ True _____ False

6 I feel stressed out most of the time.

_____ True _____ False

7 I can't remember the last time I used all my allotted vacation and personal days.

_____ True _____ False

8 It sometimes feels as though I never even have a chance to catch my breath before I have to move on to the next project/ crisis.

_____ True _____ False

9 I can't recall the last time I read – and finished – a book that I was reading purely for pleasure.

_____ True _____ False

10 I wish I had more time for outside interests and hobbies, but I simply don't.

_____ True _____ False

11 I often feel exhausted – even early in the week.

_____ True _____ False

12 I can't remember the last time I went to the movies or visited a museum or attended some other cultural event.

_____ True _____ False

13 I do what I do because so many people (children, partners, parents) depend on me for support.

_____ True _____ False

14 I've missed many of my family's important events because of work-related time pressures and responsibilities.

_____ True _____ False

15 I almost always bring work home with me.

_____ True _____ False

Look over the fifteen statements. Select three that you will work on to begin to bring healthy balance into your life.

1 _____

2 _____

3 _____

Foundation for Work Life Balance is Values Clarity

The keystone to knowing yourself is your values. All choices or trade-offs are based on your values. The majority of our stress and unhappiness is a result of believing and valuing one thing and, yet, finding yourself doing another. Only when your values and your activities are congruent – like a hand in a glove – do you feel happy and at peace with yourself

Why is it important to know what your values are? Simple –so you can make better choices.

People who don't know their values tend to wander around,

bouncing from one thing to another, trying to find themselves. They're like puppets, pulled along without any clear direction.

Knowing your values helps you:

Follow a clear set of rules and guidelines for your actions. You are less likely to take the easy way out or chase after short-term gains at the expense of your long-term goals if you've identified your values.

Make good decisions. You quickly recognize what are the good choices for you and what alternatives are not.

Find compatible people, places, and things that support your way of living.

Live with integrity. Integrity here doesn't simply mean honesty or authenticity. Integrity is the alignment of your values and your behavior. It is a clear understanding and commitment to do what you value most. Integrity means wholeness or completeness. It means being a whole person with nothing left out as you act in a manner true to yourself and your values.

Know Yourself

You might start determining your basic values by answering a few key questions:

*How would you spend your life if you learned today that
        you had only six months to live?*
*If you were going to enjoy perfect health for the next six months
        and then die from an incurable illness, how would you
        organize your time?*
Who would you want to spend your time with?
What would you want to accomplish?
What would you like to leave behind?
*How would you like to be remembered, and who would
        you like to be remembered by?*

Charles Garfield, the author of *Peak Performance*, once said that you are not really ready to live until you know what you would do with your last hour on earth. This is a values question and requires a values analysis. Your answers to the six questions listed above will give you a pretty good indication of what is really important to you in life. And, invariably, you will find that people in your life immediately spring to mind.

You've heard it said that no businessperson on his deathbed ever said that he wished that he had spent more time at the office. When your time is limited, even in your imagination, your mind clears wonderfully, and you are enabled to see the things you need to do to achieve a higher quality of life.

So knowing yourself means knowing what you truly value and knowing what is really important to you. The complete man or woman decides what is right before he decides what is possible. The balanced individual organizes his or her life to assure that everything that he or she is doing is consistent with his or her true values. It is essential for you to organize your life around your values, rather than to organize your life around the demands of your external world. This creates a reactionary lifestyle driven by the demands of the moment, rather than a responsive lifestyle driven by values.

Values Action Steps

Once your values and the integrity that drives those values are aligned, here are some guidelines to help you develop specific behaviors.

1. Align your personal or professional goals with your values.

The starting point to alleviate the pressure and stress in your life is to stop and think. Most people are so busy rushing back and forth that they seldom take the time to think seriously about who they are and why they are doing what they are doing. They engage in frantic activity, instead of thoughtful analysis. Perhaps it was this type of hectic lifestyle that caused Aristotle to observe: "The unexamined life isn't worth living."

Stop and think about a harmonious alignment (balance) of your values and your goals. Don't be like the frustrated individual who commented: "I was so busy climbing the ladder of success that when I got to the top, I realized it was leaning against the wrong wall!"

2. Prioritize your priorities.

After you have a harmonious alignment (balance) of your values and goals, the next step is to set your priorities. Make a list of all the things that you could possibly do and then select from that list the things that are most important to you based on what you know about yourself, others and your responsibilities. Part of the maturity process is letting go of nice, even fun and perhaps valuable activities in order to pursue more worthwhile goals. What items or pursuits are you hanging on to?

Keep an activity log. Track everything you do for one week. Include both work related and non work related activities. Decide what is necessary and what brings you the most satisfaction. Cut or delegate activities you don't enjoy or don't have time for.

If you don't have the authority to make certain decisions, talk to the person that does. Provide reasons that won't downgrade the activity you're giving up. It's not that the endeavor is insignificant but, based on your values prioritization it simply didn't make the cut.

3. Define what *balance* means to you.

Balance has nothing to do with a 50/50 arrangement or clock time. It doesn't mean that for every hour of work, you must have an hour off-work. It has to do with how we use the time we have. It means finding what is *a reasonable balance for you.*

Is it a few hours a week unencumbered by work concerns? Perhaps it's some solitude before bedtime? Is it playing with your kids more? Is it having an actual conversation with your significant other each day? Maybe it's a community, religious or sports activity that you're passionate about? Schedule those events and structure them into your life. It is up to you to define what balance means as you incorporate your significant relationships into the definition.

4. Structure your off-work activities.
In a study of work/life balance at AT&T of busy, high-potential professionals, this was a major finding! It may seem counterintuitive, but the best adjusted people force themselves to structure off-work activities just as much as they do work activities. Otherwise your work will drive everything else out.

5. Leverage your work strength in your personal life.
One tactic that helps is for people to use their work strengths in their off work life. What makes your work life successful? If you are organized; manage, arrange or coordinate something at home. If you are very personable, use your people skills. As commonsensical as this may seem, work life balance studies find that people with poor off-work lives do not use their strengths while they are not at work. They simply left those skills at the office.

6. Practice being in the present.
Concentrate on the present. Busy people with not much time learn to get into the present tense without carrying the rest of their concerns and deadlines with them. When you have only one hour to relax, exercise or play with the kids ... be there! Have fun. Besides, you won't solve any problems during those 60 minutes away. Train your mind to be where you are. Focus on the moment. Wherever you are, be there!

To balance your work, marriage and family is not easy, but it's not impossible. It will take intentional, disciplined and determined effort to develop and execute a plan that will work for you.

Marriage Vision:
Keep Your Marriage Ignited

"Not much happens without a dream.
And for something great to happen, there must
be a great dream. Behind every great achievement
is a dreamer of great dreams."
– ROBERT GREENLEAF

It's your 50th wedding anniversary. Your kids, grandchildren, and friends are eagerly waiting to hear a word from you about your five decades of marriage. You give an empathetic glance to each other, clear your throat, brush back a tear, and say ....

What *would* you say? What *was* your marriage about? How could you sum up your life together in a few sentences?

In helping couples write their marriage vision, I ask them to live that moment – and tell me what they would say to their kids on their 50th wedding anniversary.

"Happy anniversary and thank you," won't do. This should be something personal ... something that could guide, encourage, and strengthen them along the way as they are becoming couples and parents. I ask them to take turns listening to one another in order to truly understand their spouse's hopes, dreams, and vision for their marriage and family.

This is what couples have said:

"We made it because we were willing to work and not give up. We were willing to persevere and be such great friends."

"I would say I chose the right person. I've been so happy — with all the men that are out there in the world, I chose the one that's perfect for me. He is my best friend. I think about him when I'm at home alone, and I can't wait to talk to him when he comes home."

"It was not easy. We had a lot of trials, laughs, and time spent getting to know each other and learning to trust. It was our commitment to one another and our marriage vows that enabled us to reach 50 years."

In coaching with business leaders, time is spent in the first couple of sessions thinking about the future of their organization. Then we explore how a specific vision can make those dreams an eventual reality. Strategic planning literature suggests that businesses need to have two organizations going simultaneously: one that implements the current business plan and one that is creating the business plan of the future.

The vision of what the enterprise will be in the future creates a clear and distinct mental image – a blueprint in the mind's eye. The vision excites the imagination.

But vision is more than just hope or imagination. Vision is potential that can one day become a reality. It triggers a process in the brain that begins to identify and garner resources to turn the vision into a reality. The filament in the electric light bulb, the tiny chip that powers your iPhone, and even the footprints on the moon all began with unique visions that became reality.

Vision Quest

Native American cultures, as well as others around the world, have a tradition of the *Vision Quest* – a turning point in which they find the meaning for their lives; through a ritual process they examine their future in order to discover their purpose. It is thought that this prepares them fully for the challenges they will face.

Although I'm not suggesting you go into the wilderness and meditate for weeks, it should be understood that an essential success principle is giving life and work a sense of meaning by casting a captivating vision. Vision fuels the commitment essential to pressing on in spite of difficult relational upsets.

How Vision Saved My Family

I had rented a Jeep in the Rocky Mountain mining town of Silverton, Colorado. The day was bright and sunny as we bumped along a narrow mining road at 10,500 feet. There was a wall of mountains on our left. To our right, there was a steep cliff overlooking a beautiful valley. We were drinking in the majesty of the Rockies without a care in the world.

Suddenly, a summer rainstorm appeared out of nowhere and we were engulfed in a blanket of clouds, rain, and hail. I slowed the Jeep to a crawl and immediately flipped on my lights. I grabbed the steering wheel with both hands as I tensed up. The beautiful vistas were gone, replaced with zero visibility. All we could see was the front of our Jeep and a foot of road ahead. My kids were screaming in terror. My wife was crying. And I realized that at any moment we could roll over the cliff and all be killed.

After a couple of minutes of paralyzing fear, the storm quickly blew past onto the next range, and the vision of where we were going was restored. Everyone calmed down and we continued our high country experience.

In a very powerful and personal way that brought home to me the importance of having a vision. There are going to be times in your marriage when a storm can threaten its survival. Although storms can be intense, they are rarely permanent. Your vision will keep your focus on where you're going instead of the relational turbulence of the moment.

Your Personal Vision Quest

A Marriage Vision is essential. Here's how a vision helps your marriage:

1. A vision *inspires* you to grow.
Nothing motivates people like envisioning a positive future. Vision inspires you to work through the problems in your marriage. It gives you strength to deal with the tough issues of forgiving yourself, forgiving your spouse, and forgetting the hurts of the past. It gives hope when you feel hopeless.

2. A vision brings *unity*.
Defining a marital vision helps both of you to get on the same page. I often ask couples to take out separate sheets of paper and write this question at the top: "What is our marriage all about?" Many couples are shocked to learn they have completely different visions for their marriage. A lack of vision clarity and unity is at the core of much conflict in marriage.

3. A vision brings *direction* to you as a couple.
When you clarify your marital vision, you're laying the blueprint for a great marriage. Marriage is a journey. Both of you need to sit down and talk with each other about where you're going and how you're going to get there. A marital vision provides this common direction.

Your *Marriage Vision* is a dynamic word picture that gives direction to the marriage of your dreams. This vision excites the imagination to believe that what is merely a vision of your marriage can one day become a reality.

Three Vision Musts

For your *Marriage Vision* to be effective, it must have at least three characteristics. It must be: *positive, grounded*, and *specific*.

Positive

Your vision statement is a positive word picture of the marriage of your dreams. It should not contain negative or corrective statements about the current condition of your marriage. A vision paints a positive and compelling vision of what your marriage is becoming. Hope is the energy that will propel your marriage into the future. Your vision statement is the delivery system that injects hope into the engine of your marriage.

As you write your statement, it needs to be both positive and compelling enough to sustain you as you do the hard work required to get your marriage from here to there. Your vision will provide the stability to help you navigate through all the setbacks you'll encounter along the way.

Your present marriage condition may make a positive image of the future seem unattainable. It may be a real stretch for you and your spouse to imagine a positive future – but that's precisely why you need a vision. Your *Marriage Vision Quest* will help clarify and see mentally what you want, but don't currently have.

Grounded

One of the purposes of this book is to prepare you to create and write down your marriage vision. The self-assessments and questions have been designed to help you avoid pie in the sky ideas regarding marriage that are divorced from the reality of your current relational challenges. You are now ready to write a vision that keeps your marriage relationship ignited and continuously growing.

Remember, a vision is something that you picture in the future, not a current reality. You must be aware of where you are in order to get to where you want to go. By keeping your eye on the future and concentrating your energy on the present, your vision of the future provides the motivation and energy to help you effectively deal with current relational struggles.

Specific

Friendship, romance, and passion are aspects of a healthy marriage relationship, but they're vague in terms of the specifics of marriage vision. An effective vision may be literary in quality and inspirational in tone, but it must also be specific.

What specific need-meeting behaviors will drive friendship, romance, and passion in your marriage? Going forward, you need to identify what you will be doing in order to create friendship, romance, and passion.

Use Rudyard Kipling's six honest serving men (from *The Elephant's Child*) in creating specifics in your vision statement,

I keep six honest serving men. They taught me all I knew.

Their names are

What and
Why and
When and
How and
Where and
Who

Beginning Your Personal Vision Quest:

A positive, grounded, and specific marriage vision is created by asking specific questions:

What are the five things you most enjoy doing as a couple? (These are the things that, without which, your weeks, months, and years would feel incomplete.)

What three things must you do every single day to experience the feelings of fulfillment in your marriage?

Your life has a number of important facets or dimensions, all of which deserve some attention as they relate to your marriage vision statement. How do these fit into your marriage vision statement: physical, spiritual, work or career, family, social relationships, financial security, mental improvement, and attention and fun?

If it's you standing up to speak on your 50th anniversary, what will you regret not having done, seen, or achieved as a couple?

What strengths have other people observed and commented on about your marriage? What strengths do you see in your marriage?

What weaknesses have other people noticed and commented on about your marriage? What do you believe are your weaknesses?

If you're standing up to speak on your 50th anniversary, what sentence would capture the essence of your marriage?

Remember the following two guidelines:

1 When writing your vision, do so in the present tense with statements that are positive, grounded and specific.

2 A vision statement is living – that means it can and should change as you and your love for one another grows. Your marriage has two vision dynamics going on simultaneously, one that implements current vision strategies and one that is constantly planning for the future.

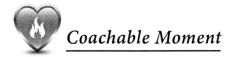 *Coachable Moment*

Okay, it's time to begin your *Marriage Vision Quest* and write your first vision draft. Put the book down and take time to think through your statement. Honestly, this may take a couple of days. Remember, without vision, your marriage will lack unity, inspiration, and direction. A vision statement is living and should change as your love for one another grows. Take time on an annual basis to read through your vision and make necessary tweaks to keep it real as you both grow in your love for one another.

Epilogue
Parting Thoughts
from the Coach

"Throughout the centuries there were men who took first steps, down new roads, armed with nothing but their own vision."
– Ann Ryan

"*I*mpossible,*"* is not a word you want to hear when it comes to saving your marriage. However, it's a word I often hear in the initial coaching session with couples.

Maybe that's been your thinking about your marriage.

Remember Caleb and Lisa Jared from the introduction?

"We look good to everyone on the outside, but at home it's a different story ... constant sarcasm, criticism, and little, if any sex," said Caleb.

Lisa added: "We spend the best part of our energy and time 'out there' and have little to give to one another."

Here's the rest of their story.

Oh, one thing I didn't mention earlier ... both of the Jared's had been involved in an affair. As a result, they believed their marriage was over and would be *impossible* to turn around. But to placate their conscience that they tried to save their marriage, they came to see me.

The enormity of their pride, pain, hurt, and anger made them one of the most challenging couples I've coached. It took a couple of weeks before they acknowledged the "unaware self" behaviors that had slowly drained the feelings of love from their marriage. Once they owned their part in their failed marriage, Caleb and Lisa were able to begin the challenging work of forgiving one another and acknowledging to the other the pain their actions had caused.

With honest self-reflection, patience, discipline and the effort of creating a work-life balance that worked for them, Lisa and Caleb turned their impossible marriage failure around.

In our final coaching session, Lisa said, "I thought what Caleb and I once had was gone forever! Over the past months as we worked to turn things around, there were times when I thought our marriage was hopeless, but I hung in there. I almost didn't get past being able to forgive Caleb … I had some deep emotional scars. But I was eventually able to let go of my pain and anger and forgive him. I now understand what married love is about and the responsibility I have in keeping the feelings of being in love alive in our marriage."

Caleb commented: "I'll ditto what Lisa said. For me, one of the hardest things to get past was my pride. My business is very successful, but my marriage was an absolute failure! To admit that and to also accept that I had a big part in that failure wasn't easy for me. It took some time for the information on self-awareness to sink in, but once it did, I began to take the necessary steps to turn our marriage around by changing myself first."

If the Jared's were able to turn their impossible marriage around, *you can too!*

Careers, kids, laser-lane life style, and personal struggles — these are the ingredients that create the drift in a marriage that slowly leads to emotional emptiness, affairs and divorce. The behaviors of committed love keep the feelings of love alive and well.

It's when there is a lack of understanding, intentional effort and discipline to practice the behaviors of *married love*, couples end up in my office saying, "We love one another but we are not in love with one another." What they mean is, "The strong emotional connection we once had is gone."

When emotions falter, couples often begin to fantasize about other relationships that will give them the emotional high they once had. What they fail to realize is that the emotional high of a new relationship will also cool. The consistent practice of committed love will keep the feeling of love alive and well, but never to the extent of the emotional high of those early days of the relationship. As *married love* matures, feelings of being "in love," the pleasures of sexual chemistry, and being connected as best friends, are part of an "until death do us part" relationship.

By combining your *Married Love Plan* with an intentional, consistent, and disciplined effort to drive the behaviors of *married love*, you will keep the feelings of being in love alive and you will have a "happily ever after marriage."

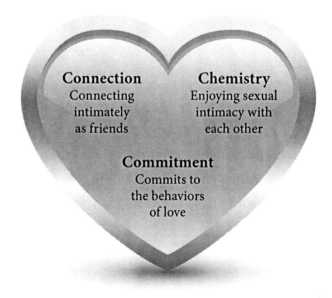

Connection
Connecting
intimately
as friends

Chemistry
Enjoying sexual
intimacy with
each other

Commitment
Commits to
the behaviors
of love

About the Author

M*ike Danchak,* the founder of *The Cutting Edge,* is a popular counselor and coach specializing in professional development and marriage coaching.

As a licensed marriage and family therapist, licensed counselor and certified professional development coach, his widespread experience includes business leadership, counseling in the public schools, church ministry, EPA consulting, corporate development coaching as well as having served as President of the Frio Hospital Association.

Mike is passionate about healthy marriages and families and working in the Dallas-Fort Worth metropolitan area has allowed him to coach couples from diverse cultural and professional backgrounds. Drawing from these broad experiences and coupled with his comprehensive training, Mike has developed the highly successful *Married Love Plan,* an interactive coaching approach designed to strengthen and promote healthy marriages.

Danchak is a highly sought after speaker at corporate, community and religious venues. His public involvement has included hosting a daily radio program as well as having written a weekly newspaper column. Currently, his influence extends through seminars, workshops, keynotes and the highly acclaimed *Tighter Knot* DVD series.

Mike and his wife Sharon partner together for pre-marital coaching, staff development seminars for preschool and elementary educators and *Love and Logic* parenting classes. The Danchaks have an adult son and daughter and four grandchildren.

Find out more about Mike's background and experience by connecting with him on LinkedIn. To discover how he can partner with you or your organization, visit his website at www.MikeDanchak.com.

CPSIA information can be obtained at www.ICGtesting.com
Printed in the USA
LVOW080321010313

322219LV00003B/183/P